Roads to

Edited by Alex Cha......

Sound Money Project

A Project of the Atlas Economic Research Foundation

Roads to Sound Money

Copyedited by Theodore Phalan
Cover Design by David Kennedy

For information and other requests, please write:
Atlas Economic Research Foundation
1201 L St NW, Second Floor
Washington, DC 20005
Atlasnetwork.org

ISBN: 978-0-615-70131-8

Printed in the United States of America

This publication was made possible with generous funding from the Searle Freedom Trust.

Table of Contents

Foreword

While the United States still goes through a frail and feeble economic recovery and the Euro faces severe problems of its own, monetary policy ought to be one of the first items in the economic reform agenda. At a time when the Federal Reserve continues to engage in unprecedented discretionary behavior and the United States faces a fiscal cliff, the message that the nine contributors to this book are trying to convey is more important than ever.

There is no way around the fact that money is half of all transactions. This simply means that when you engage in a mutually beneficial exchange, whether it be buying or selling a product or service, what you give or get in return is money. In current monetary debates, the fundamental purpose of money is largely forgotten; wholly discretionary actions are taken by the Fed to manipulate money and affect the value of the dollar without regard for money's true essence. The link between money and the real economy is broken, and although there are many factors in play, policymakers and central bankers are affecting entrepreneurs in ways that curtail effective decision making. The result is to stymie economic growth in the present and to reduce the prospects for prosperity in the future.

Predictability is an important factor for economic participants, allowing entrepreneurs to make long-term business plans. An economy based on a solid monetary foundation reduces uncertainty, resulting in more dynamic real activity and greater resilience to downturns. That is what is missing in our current monetary system, both in the US and internationally. A fix is in order but it shouldn't mean more bailouts, quantitative easing or other short-term solutions. The time has come to grapple with the tough decisions that lie ahead and consider solutions and reforms not aimed at benefiting the privileged financial sector but rather focused on serving the needs of producers and consumers in the real economy.

The authors in this book analyze the current monetary regime, both at home and abroad, to address these issues. Together, their contributions provide lessons taken from monetary history and offer proposals for long-term reform that will help to restore the morality of money, to reaffirm its essence.

In the first chapter, Dr. Jerry O'Driscoll discusses the current international monetary system through a historical lens showing the negative effects of monetary nationalism as well as the need to downsize government as a way to achieve sound money. Steven Hanke, Allan Meltzer and George Selgin analyze the Federal Reserve's behavior and policies and put forward serious recommendations for reforming the system.

Lew Lehrman provides a compelling case for a return to the Gold Standard, and Larry White describes a way to implement free banking in the US based on a Gold Standard. Jerry Jordan explains the link between fiscal and monetary policy, laying out solutions for improving fiscal policy as the antecedent for improved monetary policy.

Sean Fieler provides a description of the link between monetary policy and financial markets, and as a final chapter, Alex Chafuen addresses the morality of money in the context of defining the soundness of money across nations.

All of these contributions serve to provide a broad spectrum of proposals for improving the current monetary system – but even more, they lay the groundwork for more sweeping reforms. The Atlas Economic Research Foundation is pleased to further the aims of the Sound Money Project through this compendium of insightful perspectives and innovative recommendations. We are delighted to have partnered with these eminent authors and hope their thoughtful suggestions will enliven the debate on the need for broad monetary reform. The ideas presented herein should be discussed in further detail so that we can move vigorously forward toward the goal of achieving sound money.

Dr. Judy Shelton
Director, Sound Money Project

Toward a Global Monetary Order

Gerald P. O'Driscoll Jr.[1]

> Throughout virtually all of human history, up until 1971, money was some form of valuable and durable commodity, or a claim on such a commodity.
> —Steil and Hinds (2009: 67–68)

I will begin by disputing that there is a global monetary system. We do not have a system in any meaningful sense. There are 182 independent currencies in the world. Some currencies are fixed in relation to other, larger currencies (e.g., the Hong Kong dollar to the U.S. dollar). Some currencies move within a band against other currencies (e.g., the Singapore dollar and the Chinese yuan). Many currencies float on foreign exchange markets, but few float freely. Four major currencies float against each other: the U.S. dollar, the euro, the pound, and the yen. Countries also change their foreign exchange regime (e.g., Mexico in recent decades).

The multiplicity and changeability of arrangements defies the use of "system," certainly not in comparison to arrangements of the past or possible arrangements of the future. Stability and certainty of expectations are not possible. The dollar still dominates, and one might suggest that "the Fed rules." But the Federal Reserve follows no rule, and is not the source of stability or certainty.

No one designed the global fiat monetary arrangements; the world stumbled into them. Global fiat money came about because of flaw in the prior global monetary arrangements and political considerations in the United States.

There certainly were advocates for the current system. They believed that fiat monies would work better than the gold standard. The problem is that all the supposed advantages have proved elusive, and the predicted deficiencies have been realized in practice. The issues were debated in the 1930s, and that debate remains surprisingly modern.

1 *Cato Journal*, Vol. 32, No. 2 (Spring/Summer 2012). Copyright © Cato Institute. All rights reserved.

Monetary Nationalism

The theory behind current global monetary arrangements is monetary nationalism. It argues that each country should have its own money, and that the size of the national money stock should *not* be determined in the same way that money is distributed in different regions within a country. In the case of the United States, trade and capital flows among the states determine the share of the total money supply held by residents in each state. A truly global monetary order would work the same way across countries. That was basically how the classical gold standard worked in the 19th century (Hayek 1937: 4).

The world has not experienced the operation of the classical gold standard since the eve of World War I. Countries suspended convertibility during the war, that is, they denied their citizens and foreigners the opportunity to exchange national currencies for gold. Central banks financed government wartime spending by printing money. Consequently, prices rose.

After the war, there were price deflations of varying magnitudes. These were exacerbated by the decision of some countries, notably the United Kingdom, to return to gold convertibility at the prewar parity. Economists as diverse as Ludwig von Mises and John Maynard Keynes, as had David Ricardo 100 years before, advised against the return to convertibility at prewar parity. Their advice was ignored (Hayek 1937: 44).

The post-WWI system was a form of the gold-exchange standard. Central banks economized on their gold reserves, which created chronic payments problems among the central banks. Creditor countries were pressured not to demand gold reserves from debtor countries (Meltzer 2003: 137–270). *The fundamental problem was not gold, but its undervaluation relative to national currencies.*

The amount of undervaluation differed in different countries. Gold constrained but did not determine the supply of national currencies. There were already elements of monetary nationalism within the system. Gold flows were often "sterilized"—that is, offset by changes in national money supplies independent of the gold flows (Friedman and Schwartz 1963: 284–85, 291).

The system collapsed in the wake of the Great Depression. Country after country suspended convertibility. In the past, such suspensions were limited to wartime and viewed as temporary. In the 1930s, the breakdown of international trade and investment flows mimicked what happens in wartime. Some view that breakdown as prelude to the next war.

The world (or at least the United States and Europe) found itself with fiat currencies. The question was whether there would be a return to a gold standard. There were efforts for such a return. Some economists preferred to make virtue out of necessity and made the case for monetary nationalism as the new global monetary system.

Monetary nationalists thought the system would produce a number of benefits. Avoiding price deflation loomed large, and Hayek (1937: 7–8) regarded that "as the only argument on which the case for monetary nationalism can be rationally based." Fear of deflation, then as now, is a dominant concern. But it is surely suspect, as the example of the United States illustrates.

Money flows constantly among the 50 states, redistributing shares of the national money supply. Scarcely anyone knows it is happening (White 1998: 394; Steil and Hinds 2009: 95–96). Importantly for this discussion, changes in the share of the national money supply do not produce regional or state inflations and deflations. Prices, at least of traded goods, are left unaffected. The money flows effect changes in the geographic distribution of real resources. And that is how a truly international monetary system would work.[2]

There were periods of sustained deflation in the 19th century. They were associated, however, with technological progress and associated productivity growth. In both the United Kingdom and the United States, economic growth occurred along with falling prices. Between 1873 and 1913, Britain experienced growth in real income of 65 percent while prices fell 20 percent on average. In the United States, the income gain was 110 percent while prices fell 32 percent (Steil and Hinds 2009: 167–68).

---

2 White (1998) outlines a system of "monetary internationalism" in which there is not only an international base money (gold) but also transnational fiduciary money (bank notes and deposits) with global branch banking

In the 1870s, Friedman (1992: 113) notes, "Prices came down as rapidly as they did only because output was rising so much faster than the quantity of money was." Friedman and Schwartz (1963: 15) observed that the historical record "casts serious doubts on the validity of the now widely held view that secular price deflation and rapid economic growth are incompatible." They also found there were periods of decelerations in the rate of economic growth (from approximately 1892 to 1896), followed by sharp accelerations (1896–1901). But there was growth over the entire period 1879–1914. Friedman and Schwartz (1963: 93) conclude "that the forces making for economic growth over the course of several business cycles are largely independent of the secular trend in prices."

In the United Kingdom for the period from resumption after the Napoleonic Wars to the eve of WWI, the price level was roughly unchanged. True long-run price stability is a major economic benefit of the gold standard. The deflationary episodes in the 19th century reflected the conflux of two events: extremely rapid economic growth and the international spread of the gold standard. As countries adopted gold, the monetary demand for it increased. Technological advances in gold production and new discoveries of gold eventually enabled the supply of gold to catch up to the new global demand for gold for monetary use (Friedman 1992: 112–13).

I am making a distinction between what has been called "good" and "bad" deflation by Selgin (1997) and Horwitz (2010). Good deflation is a consequence of strong productivity growth. Goods become cheaper over time. Real wages rise because of the productivity gains. And the real value of money balances increases. Bad deflation is a consequence of monetary shocks. The causes of the two deflations are different and so, too, are the consequences. Monetary history simply does not support the view that deflation is always bad.

The idea that "deflation is bad (always)" comes from the consequences of the breakdown of the gold standard, not its operation. The major breakdown was caused by WWI, from which the system never fully recovered. The monetary shocks and unanticipated inflation of WWI were followed by what amounted to a deflationary monetary shock of returning to convertibility at prewar parities.

These were not the growth-induced secular declines in prices of the 19th century.

And then there was the experience of the Great Depression. Friedman and Schwartz (1963) argued that the Fed permitted the money supply to collapse. It is an explanation now broadly accepted. The return to the gold standard at the wrong parities and policy errors of central banks were to blame. As I have noted, central banks could and did exercise discretion under the gold-exchange standard.

Fiat money and flexible exchange rates are supposed to insulate countries from the transmission of financial shocks. They obviously have not done so. It is instructive to understand why. Hayek (1937:56) diagnosed why they would not work as promised. The "variability of exchange rates introduces a new and powerful reason for short-term capital movements." The fear of depreciation in an exchange rate drives capital out of that currency, while the expectation of an appreciation in a currency attracts capital into assets denominated in that currency. Such movements can be self- reinforcing, leading to large swings in exchange rates. It is a scenario that has been repeated many times since Hayek predicted them.

It is worth dwelling on the issue. First, and contrary to popular mythology, capital flows in the 19th and early 20th centuries were proportionately *higher* than today. According to Steil and Hinds (2009: 93), "Mean current account surpluses and deficits as a percentage of GDP in 1880 were roughly twice as high as they are today. British foreign net investment reached 7.7 percent of GDP in 1872, and a high of 8.7 percent in 1911—nearly twice Japan and Germany peaks in the late 1980s."

What separates the gold standard from monetary nationalism is that short-term capital movements were stabilizing in the classical gold standard while, as Hayek predicted, they can be destabilizing with fiat currencies. For the gold standard, Steil and Hinds (2009:95) explain the mechanism: "Trade deficits not offset by an inflow of long-term capital could be reliably financed by short-term inflows stimulated by a modest rise in short-term interest rates. The cross-border flow of gold itself was peripheral to the adjustment mechanism."

Bretton Woods

The 1930s witnessed a collapse of global trade and capital flows. Currency blocks formed within which trade occurred behind protective tariffs (Friedman and Schwartz 1963: 315, 315n). Monetary nationalism, including competitive currency depreciations, was associated with the decline in global trade and investment. The allies, particularly the United States and Great Britain, were determined that post- WWII international institutions would avoid the beggarthy-neighbor policies of the 1930s. The Bretton Woods system of international organizations and its monetary arrangements was the outcome. Meltzer (2003: 612–27) and Eichengreen (2011: 45–51) provide historical accounts.

The Bretton Woods monetary system envisioned fixed exchange rates with a gold linkage. All other member countries linked to the U.S. dollar with the dollar linked to gold. The gold linkage was even more tenuous than with the post-WWI gold exchange standard. The economizing on gold reserves was even greater. It was truly a dollar standard with the ghost of gold.

It worked as long as it did because, at the end of World War II, there was a dollar shortage among trading partners. Countries needed dollars, which constituted international reserves, to grow and rebuild their economies. They accumulated dollars through trade and by attracting long-term investment. By the end of the 1950s, however, the global dollar shortage had ended. As Eichengreen (2011:49) wryly observes, "This was not an entirely happy development." The inner contradictions of Bretton Woods were now revealed.

Bretton Woods depended on the United States running chronic balance of payments deficits in order to provide global liquidity. When the dollar shortage ended, however, the United States continued to flood the world with dollars. The link to gold was fixed at $35 per ounce. The supply of dollars was elastic and the supply of gold was inelastic. To continue to function, foreign holders of dollars had to be persuaded not to demand gold for their dollars (Eichengreen 2011: 49–50; Steil and Hinds 2009: 223–26). Such a system was bound to collapse, as had the gold-exchange standard. President Nixon's decision to close the gold window in August 1971 (i.e., permanently end the convertibility of dollars into gold) was in response to a growing international run on the dollar for gold amid rising U.S. inflation.[3]

Monetary nationalism had not won by the persuasiveness of its intellectual arguments, but by default and political tactics of a president worried about his reelection. There was no finely tuned economic calculus behind the Camp David decision. The world once again returned to fiat currencies and floating exchange rates. It was a system historically associated with wars and the temporary expedients that war begets. What followed immediately was the first peace-time high-inflation episode in the United States.

Longer-term, the pure fiat money system exposed the rest of the world to what Steil and Hinds (2009: 200) term a monetary conflict of interest within the Fed: "The money it creates is both a domestic currency and international one, and the objectives of each of the aspects of the dual role can and frequently do clash." The legacy today is a Fed policy that is increasingly viewed as a beggar-thy-neighbor policy to gain competitive advantage for its exporters. It is a return to the 1930s.

The Way Forward

Steil and Hinds (2009) emphasize that the gold standard was the monetary system compatible with the classical liberal order— namely, with free trade and free capital movements. That order worked because governments were much smaller than today (about 10 percent of GDP). This realization led Steil and Hinds (2009: 239–39) to shy away from the logic of their own argument, which is a return to the gold standard. In much the same fashion, Hayek (1937) deferred to what he thought was politically possible and did not follow his own logic.

I don't know what is politically possible, nor do most economists. There is nothing in the training of economists that provides that expertise. I do know that economic freedom and political freedom are systematically related. To maintain the classical liberal order requires the monetary arrangements congruent with that order

---

3   Meltzer (2009: 763–69) and Ferrell (2010: 50–54) provide an account of the Camp David meeting at which the decision was made (along with imposition of price and wage controls and other policies).

(O'Driscoll 2012). That system is the classical gold standard.[4]

There are many moving parts in monetary reform. Ultimately, as many thinkers in the 1930s realized, monetary reform requires reform of the banking and financial system (Hayek 1937: 76–84). My argument is that monetary reform comes first.[5] The classical gold standard has worked with a variety of different banking systems. Vera Smith (1936) provides a historical perspective from an advocate of free banking. Free banking systems, which showed considerable institutional variation, have no central bank.

In Britain, the gold standard operated with a central bank. The Bank of England was founded in 1694 and the gold standard adopted only much later. The Bank of England dominated the system. There were many commercial banks in both England and Scotland. Lawrence H. White (1984) provides historical background and an argument for the superiority of the Scottish system of free banking over the English system with central banking.

The United States adopted gold in the 1870s, but had no central bank until 1913. The banking system was highly fragmented with numerous small institutions. Branching was highly constrained if not forbidden. Banks with a national charter issued notes.

In Canada, there emerged a system of a small number of nationally branched banks with some other financial institutions (such as trust companies). The banks issued the currency and there was no central bank until 1935 (Rich 1988). The Canadian banking system survived the Great Depression without a major failure and without a central bank to act as lender of last resort[6].

The structure of the banking system matters. But adoption of the gold standard is a key for restoring monetary discipline and a free monetary order. A gold standard accomplishes two goals (1) it constrains a central bank from offsetting good, productivity-driven deflation, and (2) it makes bad deflation less possible. Yet, a gold standard doesn't solve all problems. Restoring a commodity standard is a necessary, but not a sufficient condition for monetary reform.

---

4 In principle, another commodity could substitute for gold

5 On reform of the banking system, see Selgin, Lastrapes, and White (2010).

6 The Reserve Bank of New Zealand was founded in 1934.

The argument for gold is not that it is a perfect monetary system. There is no such thing. The most basic argument for a commodity standard is a Public Choice one: it constrains the ability of the fiscal authority to spend. If there is a central bank, a commodity standard prevents the kind of wholesale monetization of government debt that is now occurring in developed countries.

A few intellectual efforts have been made toward restoration of the gold standard, such as by Todd (2004) and White (2012). It is unlikely to come about through international agreement, but it did not do so in the 19th century either (Steil and Hinds 2009: 84). Britain's adoption was a strong impetus to its gradual adoption by other countries that saw it in their self-interest to do so. It emerged as a global monetary system in an unplanned fashion.

My argument is simply that restoration of the gold (or other) commodity standard must be on the agenda for those wanting to restore a classical liberal order. Doing so undoubtedly requires greatly downsizing government. Downsizing government is its own imperative. A gold standard, by constraining central banks, would help limit the growth of government. It would also render possible a serious debate over the rationale for central banking.

References

Eichengreen, B. (2011) *Exorbitant Privilege*. New York: Oxford University Press.

Ferrell, R. H. (ed.) (2010) *Inside the Nixon Administration: The Secret Diary of Arthur Burns, 1969–1974*. Lawrence, Kan.: University Press of Kansas.

Friedman, M. (1992) *Money Mischief: Episodes in Monetary History*. New York: Harcourt Brace Jovanovich.

Friedman, M., and Schwartz, A. J. (1963) *A Monetary History of the United States, 1867–1960*. Princeton. N.J.: Princeton University Press.

Hayek, F. A. ([1937] 1971) *Monetary Nationalism and International Stability*. Reprint. New York: Augustus M. Kelley.

Horwitz, S. (2010) "Deflation: The Good, the Bad and the Ugly." *Freeman* 60 (January/February). Available at: www.thefreemanonline.org/featured/deflation-the-good-the-bad-and-the-ugly.

Meltzer, A. H. (2003) *A History of the Federal Reserve*, Vol. 1: 1913–1951. Chicago: University of Chicago Press.

_____ (2009) *A History of the Federal Reserve*, Vol. 2, Book 2, 1970–1986. Chicago: University of Chicago Press.

O'Driscoll, G. P. Jr. (2012) "Monetary Order for a Free Society." In S. Gregg (ed.) *Money, Economics and the Common Good: Perspectives from Natural Law*. St. Andrews Studies in Philosophy and Public Affairs. St. Andrews, UK: University of St. Andrews (forthcoming).

Rich, G. (1988) *The Cross of Gold: Money and the Canadian Business Cycle, 1867–1913*. Ottawa: Carleton University Press.

Selgin, G. A. (1997) *Less Than Zero: The Case for a Falling Price Level in a Growing Economy*. Hobart Paper No.132. London: Institute of Economic Affairs.

Selgin, G. A.; Lastrapes, W. D.; and White, L. H. (2010) "Has the Fed Been a Failure?" Cato Institute Working Paper No. 2 (December).

Smith, V. C. [(1936) 1990] *The Rationale of Central Banking and the Free Banking Alternative*. Reprint. Indianapolis: Liberty Press.

Steil,B., and Hinds, M. (2009) *Money, Markets and Sovereignty*. New Haven, Conn.: Yale University Press.

Todd, W. (ed.) (2004) *Prospects for a Resumption of the Gold Standard*. Proceedings of the E.C. Harwood Memorial Conference. Great Barrington, Mass.: American Institute for Economic Research.

White, L. H. (1984) *Free Banking in Britain: Theory, Experience, and Debate, 1800–1845*. Cambridge: Cambridge University Press.

_____ 1998)"Monetary Nationalism Reconsidered." In K. Dowd and R. H. Timberlake (eds.) Money and the Nation State, 377–401. New Brunswick, N.J.: Transaction Publishers.

_____ (2012) "Making the Transition to a New Gold Standard."*Cato Journal* 32

The Fed: The Great Enabler

Steve H. Hanke[1]

The Federal Reserve has a long history of creating aggregate demand bubbles in the United States (Niskanen 2003, 2006). In the ramp up to the Lehman Brothers' bankruptcy in September 2008, the Fed not only created a classic aggregate demand bubble, but also facilitated the spawning of many market-specific bubbles. The bubbles in the housing, equity, and commodity markets could have been easily detected by observing the price behavior in those markets, relative to changes in the more broadly based consumer price index. True to form, the Fed officials have steadfastly denied any culpability for creating the bubbles that so spectacularly burst during the Panic of 2008–09.

If all that is not enough, Fed officials, as well as other members of the money and banking establishments in the United States and elsewhere, have embraced the idea that stronger, more heavily capitalized banks are necessary to protect taxpayers from future financial storms. This embrace, which is reflected in the Bank for International Settlements' most recent capital requirement regime (Basel III) and related country-specific capital requirement mandates, represents yet another great monetary misjudgment. Indeed, in its stampede to make banks "safer", the establishment has spawned a policy-induced doom loop. Paradoxically, banks in the Eurozone, the United Kingdom, and the United States—among others—have been weakened by the imposition of new bank regulations in the middle of a slump. New bank regulations have suppressed the money supply and economic activity, rendering banks less "safe" (Hanke 2012).

Aggregate Demand Bubbles

Just what is an aggregate demand bubble? This type of bubble is created when the Fed's laxity allows aggregate demand to grow too rapidly. Specifically, an aggregate demand bubble occurs when nominal final sales to U.S. purchasers (GDP – exports + imports – change

---

1   A version of this paper was presented at The International Gottfried von Haberler Conference, Vaduz, Liechtenstein (28-29) June 2012

in inventories) exceeds a trend rate of nominal growth consistent with "moderate" inflation by a significant amount.

During the 25 years of the Greenspan-Bernanke reign at the Fed, nominal final sales grew at a 5.1 percent annual trend rate. This reflects a combination of real sales growth of 3 percent and inflation of 2.1 percent (Figure 1). But, there were deviations from the trend.

Figure 1
Final Sales to Domestic Purchasers
from 1987 to 2012 Q1 (Annual Percent Change)

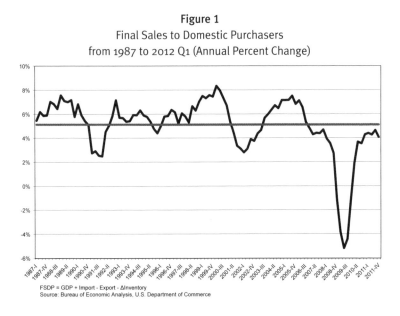

FSDP = GDP + Import - Export - ΔInventory
Source: Bureau of Economic Analysis, U.S. Department of Commerce

The first deviation began shortly after Alan Greenspan became chairman of the Fed. In response to the October 1987 stock market crash, the Fed turned on its money pump and created an aggregate demand bubble: over the next year, final sales shot up at a 7.5 percent rate, well above the trend line. Having gone too far, the Fed then lurched back in the other direction. The ensuing Fed tightening produced a mild recession in 1991.

During the 1992–97 period, growth in the nominal value of final sales was quite stable. But, successive collapses of certain Asian currencies, the Russian ruble, the Long-Term Capital Management hedge fund, and the Brazilian real triggered another excessive Fed liquidity injection. This monetary misjudgment resulted in a boom in nominal final sales and an aggregate demand bubble in 1999–2000. That bubble was followed by another round of Fed tightening, which coincided with the bursting of the equity bubble in 2000 and a slump in 2001.

The last big jump in nominal final sales was set off by the Fed's liquidity injection to fend off the false deflation scare in 2002 (Beckworth 2008). Fed Governor Ben S. Bernanke (now chairman) set off a warning siren that deflation was threatening the U.S. economy when he delivered a dense and noteworthy speech before the National Economists Club on November 21, 2002 (Bernanke 2002). Bernanke convinced his Fed colleagues that the deflation danger was lurking. As Greenspan put it, "We face new challenges in maintaining price stability, specifically to prevent inflation from falling too low" (Greenspan 2003). To fight the alleged deflation threat, the Fed pushed interest rates down sharply. By July 2003, the Fed funds rate was at a then-record low of 1 percent, where it stayed for a year. This easing produced the mother of all liquidity cycles and yet another massive demand bubble.

Artificially "low" interest rates induced investors to aggressively speculate by chasing yield in "risky" venues and to ramp-up their returns by increasing the amount of leverage they applied. These activities generated market-specific bubbles (Garrison 2011).

Over the past quarter century, and contrary to the Fed's claims, the central bank overreacted to real or perceived crises and created three demand bubbles. The last represents one bubble too many—and one that is impacting us today.

An Austrian Cycle Theme

During the Greenspan-Bernanke era the Fed has embraced the view that stability in the economy and stability in prices are mutually consistent. As long as inflation remains at or below its target level, the Fed's modus operandi is to panic at the sight of real or perceived economic trouble and provide emergency relief. It does this by pushing interest rates below where the market would have set them. With interest rates artificially low, consumers reduce savings in favor of consumption, and entrepreneurs increase their rates of investment spending.

This creates an imbalance between savings and investment, and sets the economy on an unsustainable growth path. This, in a nutshell, is the lesson of the Austrian critique of central banking. Austrian economists warned that price level stability might be inconsistent with economic stability. They placed great stress on the fact that the price level, as typically measured, extends only to goods and services. Asset prices are excluded. (The Fed's core measure for consumer prices, of course, doesn't even include all goods and services.) The Austrians concluded that monetary stability should include a dimension extending to asset prices and that changes in relative prices of various groups of goods, services and assets are of utmost importance. For the Austrians, a stable economy might be consistent with a monetary policy under which prices were gently falling (Selgin 1997).

Market-Specific Bubbles

The most recent aggregate demand bubble was not the only bubble that the Fed was facilitating. As Figure 2 shows, the Fed's favorite inflation target—the consumer price index, absent food and energy prices—was increasing at a regular, modest rate. Over the 2003–08 (Q3) period, this metric increased by 12.5 percent.

Figure 2
Relative Prices

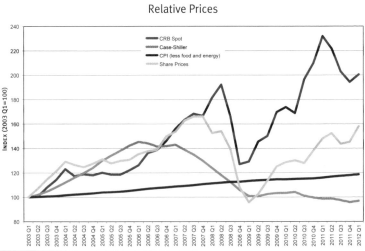

Sources: Bloomberg, Federal Reserve Bank of St. Louis, International Monetary Fund, Standard and Poor's and Author's Calculations.

The Fed's inflation metric signaled "no problems". But, as Haberler emphasized, "the relative position and change of different groups of prices are not revealed, but are hidden and submerged in a general [price] index" (Haberler 1928: 444). Unbeknownst to the Fed, abrupt shifts in major relative prices were underfoot. For any economist worth his salt (particularly Austrians), these relative price changes should have set off alarm bells. Indeed, sharp changes in relative prices are a signal that, under the deceptively smooth surface of a general price index of stable prices, basic maladjustments are occurring. And it is these maladjustments that, according to Haberler, hold the key to Austrian business cycle theory (Haberler 1986).

Just what sectors realized big swings in relative prices during the last U.S. aggregate demand bubble? Housing prices, measured by the Case-Shiller home price index, were surging, increasing by 45 percent from the first quarter in 2003 until their peak in the first quarter of 2006. Share prices were also on a tear, increasing by 66 percent from the first quarter of 2003 until they peaked in the first quarter of 2008.

The most dramatic price increases were in the commodities, however. Measured by the Commodity Research Bureau's spot index, commodity prices increased by 92 percent from the first quarter of 2003 to their pre-Lehman Brothers peak in the second quarter of 2008.

If nothing else, these dramatic swings in relative prices provides persuasive evidence that money is not neutral—a fundamental insight made by Austrian economists (Ebeling 2010). Careful research—even by non-Austrian governors of the Federal Reserve System—has verified this proposition (Maisal 1967).

The dramatic jump in commodity prices was due, in large part, to the fact that a weak dollar accompanied the mother of all liquidity cycles. Measured by the Federal Reserve's Trade-Weighted Exchange Index for major currencies, the greenback fell in value by 30.5 percent from 2003 to mid-July 2008. As every commodity trader knows, all commodities, to varying degrees, trade off changes in the value of the dollar. When the value of the dollar falls, the nominal dollar prices of internationally-traded commodities priced in dollars—like gold, rice, corn, and oil—must increase because more dollars are required to purchase the same quantity of any commodity.

Indeed, in my July 2008 testimony before the House Budget Committee on "Rising Food Prices: Budget Challenges", I estimated that the weak dollar was the major contributor to what then, only a few months before the collapse of Lehman Brothers, was viewed as the world's most urgent economic problem: world-record commodity prices. My estimates of the depreciating dollar's contribution to surging commodity prices over the 2002–July 2008 period was 51 percent for crude oil and 55.5 percent for rough rice, two commodities that set record-high prices (nominal) in July 2008 (Hanke 2008).

Before leaving the market-specific bubbles, two points merit mention. First, the relative increase in housing prices was clearly signaling a bubble in which prices were diverging from housing's fundamentals. A simple "back-of-the-envelope" calculation confirms a bubble. The so-called demographic "demand" for housing in the U.S. during the first decade of the 21st century was about 1.5 million units per year. This includes purchases of first homes by newly formed families, purchases of second homes, and the replacement of about 300,000 units per year that have been lost to fire, floods, widening of highways, and so forth (Aliber 2010).

During the bubble years of 2002–06, housing starts were two million per year. In consequence, an "excess supply" of about 500,000 units, or 25 percent of the annual new starts, was being created each year. These data suggest that housing prices in the 2002–06 period should have been very weak, or declining. Instead, they increased by 45 percent. The Fed, even according to the minutes of the Federal Open Market Committee of June 2005, failed to spot what was an all-too obvious housing bubble (Harding 2011).

The U.S. housing bubble illustrates yet another Austrian insight. For the Austrians, things go wrong when a central bank sets short-term interest rates at artificially low levels. Such rates fuel credit booms, with a decline in the discount rate pumping up the present value of capital projects. An artificially low interest rate alters the evaluation of projects – with longer-term, more capital-intensive projects becoming more attractive relative to shorter-term, less capital-intensive ones (Machlup 1935). In consequence, business-es overestimate the value of long-lived investments and an invest-ment-led boom ensues – where a plethora of investment dollars is locked up into excessively long-lived and capital-intensive projects.

Investment-led booms sow the seeds of their own destruction. The booms end in busts. These are punctuated by bankruptcies and a landscape littered with malinvestments made during the credit booms. Many of these malinvestments never see the light of day.

Austrian theory played out to perfection during the most recent boom-bust cycle. By July 2003, the Federal Reserve had pushed the federal funds interest rate down to what was then a record low of 1 percent, where it stayed for a full year. During that period, the natu-ral (or neutral) rate of interest was in the 3-4 percent range. With the fed funds rate well below the natural rate, a credit boom was off and running. And as night follows day, a bust was just around the corner.

A second point worth mentioning is that, while operating under a regime of inflation targeting and a floating U.S. dollar exchange rate, Chairman Bernanke has seen fit to ignore fluctuations in the value of the dollar. Indeed, changes in the dollar's exchange value do not appear as one of the six metrics on "Bernanke's Dashboard"—

Figure 3
USD/Euro and Commodity Prices

Source: Bloomberg

the one the chairman uses to gauge the appropriateness of monetary policy (Wessel 2009: 271). Perhaps this explains why Bernanke has been dismissive of questions suggesting that changes in the dollar's exchange value influence either commodity prices or more broad gauges of inflation (McKinnon 2010, Reddy and Blackstone 2011).

It is remarkable that the steep decline in the dollar during the 2002–July 2008 period (and associated surge in commodity prices), the subsequent surge in the dollar's value after Lehman Brothers collapsed (and associated plunge in commodity prices), and the renewed decline in the dollar's exchange rate after the first quarter of 2009 (and associated new surge in the CRB spot index – see Figure 3) has left Fed officials in denial. And if that's not enough, the dollar's exchange rate appreciated in the October 2009- June 2010 period, and the commodity bull market temporarily stalled. But, in the face of this evidence, the Fed officials continue to be stubbornly blind to the fact that there is a link between the dollar's exchange value and commodity prices (Reddy and Blackstone 2011).

More on the Fed's Dashboard Problems

In addition to not displaying the dollar's exchange rate on his dashboard, Chairman Bernanke's dashboard doesn't display money-supply gauges. This wasn't always the case. In the late summer of 1979, when Paul Volcker took the reins of the Federal Reserve System, the state of the U.S. economy's health was "bad". Indeed, 1979 ended with a double-digit inflation rate of 13.3 percent.

Chairman Volcker realized that money matters, and it didn't take him long to make his move. On Saturday, October 6, 1979, he stunned the world with an unanticipated announcement. He proclaimed that he was going to put measures of the money supply on the Fed's dashboard. For him, it was obvious that, to restore the U.S. economy to good health, inflation would have to be wrung out of the economy. And to kill inflation, the money supply would have to be controlled.

Chairman Volcker achieved his goal. By 1982, the annual rate of inflation had dropped to 3.8 percent – a great accomplishment. The problem was that the Volcker inflation squeeze brought with it a relatively short recession (less than a year) that started in January

1980, and another, more severe slump that began shortly thereafter and ended in November 1982.

Chairman Volcker's problem was that the monetary speedometer installed on his dashboard was defective. Each measure of the money supply (M1, M2, M3 and so forth) was shown on a separate gauge, with the various measures being calculated by a simple summation of their components. The components of each measure were given the same weight, implying that all of the components possessed the same degree of moneyness – usefulness in immediate transactions where money is exchanged between buyer and seller.

As shown in Figure 4, the Fed thought that the double-digit fed funds rates it was serving up were allowing it to tap on the money-supply brakes with just the right amount of pressure. In fact, if the money supply had been measured correctly by a Divisia metric, Chairman Volcker would have realized that the Fed was slamming on the brakes from 1978 until early 1982. The Fed was imposing a monetary policy that was much tighter than it thought.

Why is the Divisia metric the superior money supply measure, and why did it diverge so sharply from the Fed's conventional measure (M2)? Money takes the form of various types of financial assets

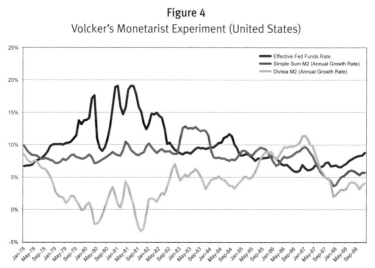

Figure 4
Volcker's Monetarist Experiment (United States)

Sources: Center for Financial Stability and the Federal Reserve Bank of St. Louis   Prof. Dr. Steve H. Hanke

that are used for transaction purposes and as a store of value. Money created by a monetary authority (notes, coins, and banks' deposits at the monetary authority) represents the underlying monetary base of an economy. This monetary base, or high-powered money, is imbued with the most moneyness of the various types of financial assets that are called money. The monetary base is ready to use in transactions in which goods and services are exchanged for "money".

In addition to the assets that make up base money, there are many others that possess varying degrees of moneyness – a characteristic which can be measured by the ease of and the opportunity costs associated with exchanging them for base money. These other assets are, in varying degrees, substitutes for money. That is why they should not receive the same weights when they are summed to obtain a broad money supply measure. Instead, those assets that are the closest substitutes for base money should receive higher weights than those that possess a lower degree of moneyness.

Now, let's come back to the huge divergences between the standard simple-sum measures of M2 that Chairman Volcker was observing and the true Divisia M2 measure. As the Fed pushed the fed funds rate up, the opportunity cost of holding cash increased. In consequence, retail money market funds and time deposits, for example, became relatively more attractive and received a lower weight when measured by a Divisia metric. Faced with a higher interest rate, people had a much stronger incentive to avoid "large" cash and checking account balances. As the fed funds rate went up, the divergence between the simple-sum and Divisia M2 measures became greater and greater.

When available, Divisia measures are the "best" measures of the money supply. But, how many classes of financial assets that possess moneyness should be added together to determine the money "supply"? This is a case in which the phrase "the more the merrier" applies. When it comes to money, the broadest measure is the "best". In the U.S., we are fortunate to have Divisia M4 available from the Center for Financial Stability in New York.

Malfeasance

For most masters of money, it is all about an inflation target. As long as they hit a target, or come close to it, they are defended from all sides by members of the establishment (Blinder 2010, Mankiw 2011). It is as if nothing else matters. The deputy governor of the world's first central bank (Sweden's Riksbank) and a well-known pioneer of inflation targeting made clear what all the inflation-targeting central bankers have in mind:

> My view is that the crisis was largely caused by factors that had very little to do with monetary policy. And my main conclusion for money policy is that flexible inflation targeting — applied in the right way and in particular using all the information about financial conditions that is relevant for the forecast of inflation and resource utilization at any horizon — remains the best-practice monetary policy before, during, and after the financial crisis [Svensson 2010: 1].

For central bankers, the "name of the game" is to blame someone else for the world's economic and financial troubles (Bernanke 2010, Greenspan 2010). How can this be, particularly when money is at the center?

To understand why the Fed's fantastic claims and denials are rarely subjected to the indignity of empirical verification, we have to look no further than the late Nobelist Milton Friedman. In a 1975 book of essays in honor of Friedman, *Capitalism and Freedom: Problems and Prospects,* Gordon Tullock (1975: 39–40) wrote:

> It should be pointed out that a very large part of the information available on most government issues originates within the government. On several occasions in my hearing (I don't know whether it is in his writing or not but I have heard him say this a number of times) Milton Friedman has pointed out that one of the basic reasons for the good press the Federal Reserve Board has had for many years has been that the Federal Reserve Board is the source of 98 percent of all writing on the Federal Reserve Board. Most government agencies have this characteristic.

Friedman's assertion has subsequently been supported by Lawrence H. White's research. In 2002, 74 percent of the articles on monetary policy published by U.S. economists in U.S.-edited journals appeared in Fed-sponsored publications, or were authored (or co-authored) by Fed staff economists (White 2005, Grim 2009).

For powerful and uncompromising dissidents, the establishment can impose what it deems to be severe penalties. For example, after the distinguished monetarist and one of the founders of the Shadow Open Market Committee, Karl Brunner, was perceived as a credible threat, he was banned from entering the premises of the Federal Reserve headquarters in Washington, D.C. Security guards were instructed to never allow Brunner to enter the building. This all backfired. Indeed, the great Swiss economist Brunner confided to Apostolos Serletis that the ban had done wonders for his career (Serletis 2006: xiii). Alas, most money and banking professionals would, unlike Brunner, find a Fed ban to be a burden they could not bear.

Military history is written by the victors. Economic history is written, to a degree, by central bankers. In both cases you have to take official accounts with a large dose of salt.

You thought you knew that the Duke of Wellington whipped Napoleon at the Battle of Waterloo. But, according to the expert on Waterloo, Peter Hofschröer, Wellington's army of 68,000 men was locked in a bloody stalemate with Napoleon's force of 73,140 until late in the afternoon of June 18, 1815 (Hofschröer 2005). That's when Field Marshall Blücher's 47,000 Prussian troops entered the field of battle and turned the tide.

The Iron Duke's official account has Prince Blücher failing to arrive until early evening and with only 8,000 troops. Somehow 39,000 Prussians simply vanished. As they say, the rest is history – literally history as written by Wellington.

Doctored accounts often gain wide circulation in the sphere of economics, too. Unfortunately, false beliefs are very difficult to overturn by facts, and fallacies play a significant role in economic policy discourse. White (2008) has masterfully shown, for example, how in an attempt to neutralize policy advice by Austrian-oriented economists, prominent Keynesian-oriented economists have simply fabricated what Hayek and Robbins had to say about economic policy during the Great Depression.

Misjudgments, Again

As part of the money and banking establishment's blame game, the accusatory finger has been pointed at commercial bankers.

The establishment asserts that banks are too risky and dangerous because they are "undercapitalized". It is, therefore, not surprising that the Bank for International Settlements located in Basel, Switzerland has issued new Basel III capital rules. These will bump banks' capital requirements up from 4 percent to 7 percent of their risk-weighted assets. And if that is not enough, the Basel Committee agreed in late June to add a 2.5 percent surcharge on top of the 7 percent requirement for banks that are deemed too-big-to-fail. For some, even these hurdles aren't high enough. The Swiss National Bank wants to impose an ultra-high 19 percent requirement on Switzerland's two largest banks, UBS and Credit Suisse (Braithwaite and Simonian 2011). In the United States, officials from the Fed and the Federal Deposit Insurance Corporation are also advocating capital surcharges for "big" banks.

The oracles of money and banking have demanded higher capital-asset ratios for banks—and that is exactly what they have received. Just look at what has happened in the United States. Since the onset of the Panic of 2008–09, U.S. banks have, under political pressure and in anticipation of Basel III, increased their capital-asset ratios (Figure 5).

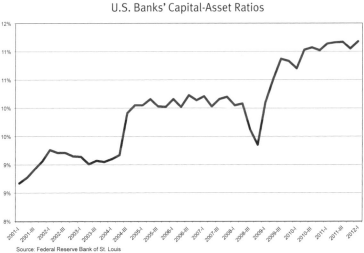

Figure 5
U.S. Banks' Capital-Asset Ratios

Source: Federal Reserve Bank of St. Louis

The oracles have erupted in cheers at the increased capital-asset ratios. They assert that more capital has made the banks stronger and safer. While at first glance that might strike one as a reasonable conclusion, it is not.

For a bank, its assets (cash, loans and securities) must equal its liabilities (capital, bonds, and liabilities which the bank owes to its shareholders and customers). In most countries, the bulk of a bank's liabilities (roughly 90 percent) are deposits. Since deposits can be used to make payments, they are "money". Accordingly, most bank liabilities are money.

To increase their capital-asset ratios, banks can either boost capital or shrink assets. If banks shrink their assets, their deposit liabilities will decline. In consequence, money balances will be destroyed. So, paradoxically, the drive to deleverage banks and to shrink their balance sheets, in the name of making banks safer, destroys money balances. This, in turn, dents company liquidity and asset prices. It also reduces spending relative to where it would have been without higher capital-asset ratios.

The other way to increase a bank's capital-asset ratio is by raising new capital. This, too, destroys money. When an investor purchases newly issued bank equity, the investor exchanges funds from a bank deposit for new shares. This reduces deposit liabilities in the banking system and wipes out money.

By pushing banks to increase their capital-asset ratios – to allegedly make banks stronger – the oracles have made their economies (and perhaps their banks) weaker (Congdon 2011). But, how could this be? After all, central banks around the world have turned on the money pumps. Shouldn't this be ratcheting up money supply growth?

The problem is that central banks only produce what Lord Keynes referred to in 1930 as "state money". And state money (also known as base or high-powered money) is a rather small portion of the total "money" in an economy. This is the case because the commercial banking system creates most of the money in the economy by creating bank deposits, or what Keynes called "bank money" (Keynes 1930).

Since August 2008, the month before Lehman Brothers collapsed, the supply of state money has more than tripled, while bank money shrunk by 12.5 percent – resulting in a decline in the total money supply (M4) of almost 2 percent (Figure 6). In consequence, the share of the total broad money supply accounted for by the Fed has jumped from 5 percent in August 2008 to 15 percent today. Accordingly, bank money as percent of the total money supply has dropped from a whopping 95 percent to 85 percent.

The disturbing course that has been taken by the money supply in the U.S. shows why we had a bubble, and why the U.S. is mired in a growth recession, at best (see Figure 7). If Fed Chairman Bernanke had a money supply indicator – any money supply indicator – on his dashboard, he would, well, see reality. Money matters.

It is clear that while Fed-produced state money has exploded, privately-produced bank money has imploded. The net result is a level of broad money that is well below where it would have been if broad money would have followed a trend rate of growth. The post-crisis monetary policy mix has brought about a massive opening of the state money-supply spigots, and a significant tightening of those in the private sector. Since bank money as a portion of the

Figure 6
State Money and Bank Money
(United States, April 2012)

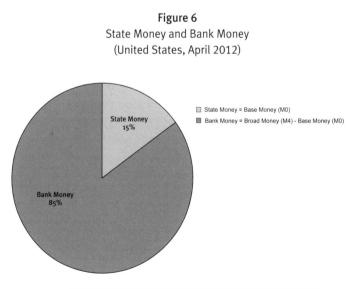

Sources: Center for Financial Stability, Federal Reserve Bank of St. Louis, and Author's Calculations

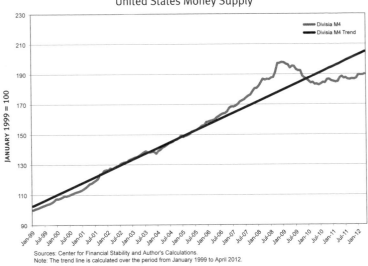

Figure 7
United States Money Supply

Sources: Center for Financial Stability and Author's Calculations.
Note: The trend line is calculated over the period from January 1999 to April 2012.

broad money supply in the U.S. is now five and a half times larger than the state portion, the result has been a decrease in the money supply since the Lehman Brothers collapse. So, when it comes to money in the U.S., policy has been, on balance, contractionary – not expansionary. This is bad news, since monetary policy dominates fiscal policy.

Wrongheaded public policies have put the kibosh on banks and so-called shadow banks, which are the primary bank money-supply engines. They have done this via new and prospective bank regulations flowing from the Dodd-Frank legislation, new (more stringent) Basel III capital and liquidity requirements, and uncertainty as to what Washington might do next. All this has resulted in financial repression – a credit crunch. No wonder we are having trouble waking up from this nightmare.

The oracles' embrace of higher capital-asset ratios for banks in the middle of the most severe slump since the Great Depression has been a great blunder. While it might have made banks temporarily "stronger", it has contributed mightily to plunging money supply metrics and very weak economic growth. Until the oracles come to

Figure 8
Holdings of U.S. Commerical Banks ($ trillion)

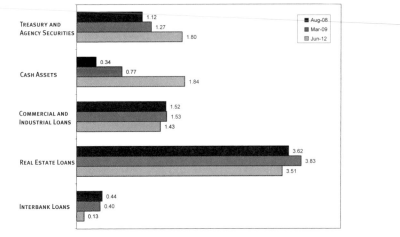

Source: Federal Reserve Board

their senses and reverse course on their demands for ever-increasing capital-asset ratios, we can expect continued weak (or contracting) money growth, economic malaise, increasing debt problems, continued market volatility, and a deteriorating state of confidence.

Conclusion

Monetary misjudgments and malfeasance have characterized U.S. policy. Artificially low Fed funds rates enabled both the aggregate and market-specific demand bubbles to be blown. Even though there were numerous signs that the financial systems in Europe and the United States were enduring severe stresses and strains in 2007, the money and banking oracles failed to anticipate and prepare for the major financial and economic turmoil that visited them in 2008–09. Indeed, the oracles' ad hoc reactions turned the turmoil into a panic. Since then, members of the money and banking establishment have been busy dissembling. They have hung out "not culpable" signs and pointed their powerful accusatory fingers at others.

The Fed has a propensity to create aggregate demand bubbles. These bubbles carry with them market-specific bubbles that distort relative prices and the structure of production. Contrary to the assertions of the stabilizers who embrace inflation targeting, these relative price distortions are potentially dangerous and disruptive.

If that was not enough, policymakers have latched onto a new mantra: to make banks "safe", higher capital requirements are absolutely essential. The banks have obliged and increased their capital-asset ratios. In consequence, the banks' loan books that are subject to higher capital-to-asset mandates (commercial and industrial loans, real estate loans and interbank loans) have shrunk (Figure 8). With that, broad money (Divisa M4) growth rates have remained submerged and a typical post-slump economic rebound has failed to materialize.

References

Aliber, R. Z. (2010) Private Correspondence (19 October).

Beckworth, D. (2008) "Aggregate Supply-Demand Deflation and Its Implications For Macroeconomic Stability." *Cato Journal* 28 (3): 363–84.

Bernanke, B. S. (2002) "Deflation: Making Sure 'It' Doesn't Happen Here." Address at the National Economists Club, Washington, D.C. (21 November).

_____ (2010) "Causes of the Recent Financial and Economic Crisis." Testimony before the Financial Crisis Inquiry Commission, Washington, D.C. (2 September).

Blinder, A. S. (2010) "In Defense of Ben Bernanke." *Wall Street Journal* (15 November).

Braithwaite, T., and Simonian, H. (2011) "Banks Make Basel Appeal to Congress." *Financial Times* (16 June).

Congdon, T. (2011) *Money in a Free Society: Keynes, Friedman, and the New Crisis in Capitalism*. New York: Encounter Books.

Ebeling, R. M. (2010) *Political Economy, Public Policy and Monetary Economics: Ludwig von Mises and the Austrian Tradition*. New York: Routledge.

Garrison, R. W. (2011) "Alchemy Leveraged: The Federal Reserve and Modern Finance." *The Independent Review* 16 (3): 435-451.

Greenspan, A. (2003) "Federal Reserve Board's Semiannual Monetary Policy Report to Congress." Committee on Financial Services, U.S. House of Representatives. Washington, D.C. (15 July).

_____ (2010) "The Crisis." *Brookings Papers on Economic Activity* (Spring): 201–46.

Grim, R. (2009) "Priceless: How the Federal Reserve Bought the Economics Profession." *Huffington Post* (7 September).

Haberler, G. (1928) "A New Index Number and its Meaning."
The Quarterly Journal of Economics 42 (3): 434-449.

_____ (1986) "Reflections on Hayek's Business Cycle Theory."
Cato Journal 6 (2): 421-435.

Hanke, S. H. (2008) "The Greenback and Commodity Prices." *Interest-Rate Outlook.*
Boston: H.C. Wainwright & Co. Economics, Inc. (11 September).

_____ (2011) "'Stronger' Banks, Weaker Economies." *Globe Asia* (August).

_____ (2012) "It's the Money Supply, Stupid." *Globe Asia* (July).

Harding, R. (2011) "Fed Misread Dangers of Housing Crash, Minutes Show."
Financial Times (14 January).

Hofschröer, P. (2005) *Wellington's Smallest Victory.* London: Faber & Faber.

Keynes, J. (1930) *A Treatise on Money, Volume I: The Pure Theory of Money.*
London: Macmillan and Co., Ltd.

Machlup, F. (1935) "The Rate of Interest as Cost Factor and as Capitalization Factor."
American Economic Review 25 (3): 459-465.

Maisal, S. J. (1967) "The Effects of Monetary Policy on Expenditures in Specific
Sectors of the Economy." *The Journal of Political Economy* 76 (4): 796-814.

Mankiw, N. G. (2011) "What's with All the Bernanke Bashing?"
New York Times (30 July).

McKinnon, R. (2010) "Rehabilitating the Unloved Dollar Standard." *Asian-Pacific
Economic Literature* 24 (2): 1–18 (April).

Niskanen, W.A. (2003) "On the Fed's Demand Bubble." *Cato Journal* 23 (1): 135–38.

_____ (2006) "An Unconventional Perspective on the Greenspan Record."
Cato Journal 26 (2): 333–35.

Reddy, S., and Blackstone, B. (2011) "Bernanke Denies that Fed is Stoking Inflation."
Wall Street Journal (4 February).

Serletis, A. (2006) *Money and the Economy.* Hackensack, N.J.: World Scientific
Publishing.

Selgin, G. (1997) *Less Than Zero: The Case for a Falling Price Level in a Growing
Economy.* Institute for Economic Analysis Hobart Papers Series No. 132. London:
Coronet Books, Inc.

Svensson, Lars. (2010) "Monetary Policy after the Financial Crisis." Address
at the Second International Journal of Central Banking Fall Conference,
Tokyo (17 September).

Tullock, G. (1975) "Discussion." In R. T. Selden (ed.) *Capitalism and Freedom:
Problems and Prospects; Proceedings of a Conference in Honor of Milton Friedman.*
Charlottesville: University Press of Virginia.

Wessel, D. (2009) *In Fed We Trust: Ben Bernanke's War on the Great Panic.*
New York: Crown Business.

White, L. H. (2005) "The Federal Reserve System's Influence on Research in Monetary Economics." *Econ Journal Watch* 2 (2): 325–54.

_____ (2008) "Did Hayek and Robbins Deepen the Great Depression." *Journal of Money, Credit and Banking* 40 (4): 751-768.

Learning about Policy from Federal Reserve History

Allan H. Meltzer[1]

For much of the past 15 years, my assistants and I have been reading minutes and papers in the National Archives, the Board of Governors, and the New York Federal Reserve Bank. I owe a debt of appreciation to the Board's librarians, to the archivists at the New York bank, to my several assistants, and to many at the Fed who cooperated helpfully to make this project come to completion[2]. The result has now been published in two volumes of more than 2,000 pages. Volume 1 covers the 1913–1951 period and has been in print several years (Meltzer 2003). Volume 2, published in February, is in two parts: part one (Meltzer 2010a) covers the 1951–69 period, and part two (Meltzer 2010b) chronicles the 1970–86 period.

In this article, I discuss some principal findings from volume 2. The starting point is the 1951 Accord with the Treasury that permitted the long-term interest rate to rise above 2.5 percent. The closing point is the end of the Great Inflation of 1986.

Volume 2 has two main themes. One is the Great Inflation. I discuss why it started, why it continued for more than 15 years, why it ended when it did, and why it has not returned, at least not yet. The second theme is the changing meaning of independence.

Much of my book is about policy errors and mistaken ideas. That is what makes the book so long. I let the principals make their arguments repeatedly to make clear that they believed in their reasons for acting as they did. Repetition reinforces my interpretations. Because I will talk about mistakes, let me start by saying a bit about achievements.

1 *Cato Journal*, Vol. 30, No. 2 (Spring/Summer 2010). Copyright © Cato Institute. All rights reserved.

2 I am indebted also to AEI for supporting the many excellent research assistants who read and summarized masses of minutes, transcripts, and staff papers; to Christopher DeMuth, who supported the project for 15 years; to Anna Schwartz, who urged me on and who commented on every chapter; and to Marilyn, my wife, who supplied much-needed emotional support and always good humor. The volumes are dedicated to those three. A special thanks to Alberta Ragan who prepared the manuscript from my hand-written pages and to the late Karl Brunner, teacher, friend, and lifetime collaborator.

The United States is the world's main monetary power. The Federal Reserve presided over the transition from a local or regional system of financial institutions to the current leader of the world monetary system. It managed the transition from the gold standard through several alternatives to the present system, or non-system, of floating rates for principal currencies. It managed the transition from a monetary arrangement based on member bank borrowing and the real bills doctrine to the present system based on open market operations supposedly directed at the dual mandate. Traditional central bank secrecy proved incompatible with democratic openness, so the Federal Reserve has learned to be more open about its operations and now concerns itself with communications policy. In its 96 years, it has remained free of major scandal. And, from the 1920s on it has done pioneering research on monetary policy and has built not one, but many, dedicated and highly qualified research staffs at the Board and several of the regional banks.

After the mistakes that produced the Great Inflation, the Federal Reserve achieved the "Great Moderation." From the mid-1980s to about 2005, the United States experienced a long period of stable growth, low inflation, and short, mild recessions. These years are the best in Federal Reserve history. Unfortunately, the System did not continue the policies that achieved its greatest success.

On the opposite side of the ledger are major and minor mistakes, many of which were repeated. Some members recognized most and perhaps all of the main errors. The Federal Open Market Committee (FOMC) minutes record all the main criticisms that I make followed by my comment saying there was no response and no discussion. Recognition by FOMC members implies that at least some of the errors could have been prevented.

Reflecting convictions held by many in Congress and in several administrations, Federal Reserve policy gave greatest attention to avoiding unemployment. It usually followed a lexicographic ordering that gave priority to employment. After most countries in Western Europe restored currency convertibility for current accounts, the conflict between the goals of the Employment Act and Bretton Woods became apparent. The Federal Reserve treated the exchange rate as a secondary or tertiary consideration, mainly a problem for the Treasury. Its main error was to diligently pursue an agreement to expand world reserves (the Triffin problem) and ignore the more pressing issue of real exchange rate adjustment. In this, it cooperated with the Treasury. I limit discussion here to domestic policy and operations.

Errors such as the failure to urge auctions of Treasury security offerings, or the greater weight given to unemployment than to inflation, or the use of 4 percent as the full employment rate long after that rate rose, reflect both error and political pressure. Economists often treat monetary policy as not affected by politics. Models of optimal monetary policy have no role for politics. Perhaps they take this position because they equate Federal Reserve independence with freedom to take action and follow any chosen path. Alas, that is rarely true. The changing meaning of "independence" is one theme of my history.

Independence

History, at least mine, tells a mixed story. In the postwar years, only part of Paul Volcker's period as chairman, 1979 to 1984, comes close to the textbook vision of independence. President Reagan appointed the majority of the Federal Reserve Board during Volcker's last years as chairman, and James Baker influenced those members. On one occasion, the Board voted 4 to 3 for a discount rate reduction that Paul Volcker opposed. And, as Treasury secretary, Baker chose an exchange rate policy that the Federal Reserve had to accept.

William McChesney Martin, Jr., defined Federal Reserve independence as "independence within the government, not independence of the government." His definition recognizes a political constraint. Martin said many times that Congress approves the budget and decides on the deficit. He thought and said the Federal Reserve had to help finance the deficit. This worked reasonably well during the Eisenhower and Kennedy presidencies when the budget was in surplus or the deficits relatively small. It produced high money growth and rising inflation during the Johnson presidency, when deficits rose. Not deficits but Federal Reserve policy of financing deficits started and sustained the Great Inflation. My history gives many other examples of political influence on the Fed.

When President Nixon appointed Arthur Burns to chair the Federal Reserve, the president left no doubt about his view of Federal Reserve independence. He told Burns and the audience that he expected the Federal Reserve to independently decide to do what he wanted done. President Nixon promised to reduce inflation without a recession. His advisers warned him that this would not happen. President Nixon said that no president is defeated for reelection because of inflation, only because of unemployment.

Burns shared his conviction. In "The Anguish of Central Banking" (1987) he explained that the Federal Reserve should have reduced money growth after 1964. They couldn't, he said, because of the political commitment to the welfare state, and the power of labor unions and business monopolies. Burns gave that speech at the 1979 International Monetary Fund meeting in Belgrade. That was the meeting Paul Volcker left early to do what Burns said could not be done.

William Miller followed Burns as chairman. He knew very little about making monetary policy. His main contribution was negotiating an agreement with Congress to end Regulation Q ceilings. The Carter administration wanted a chairman who was more cooperative than Burns. Maintaining independence was not an important concern.

The Federal Reserve has much less independence than the European Central Bank because the government of the European Union has a much smaller role in monetary policy than the U.S. administration and Congress. Congress can change the rules under which the Federal Reserve operates, and it proposes to do so frequently. Federal Reserve officials are very aware of this limit on their actions. Economists cannot understand Federal Reserve policy if they ignore political influences.

Central bank independence became explicit under the gold standard. That standard constrained monetary policy and inflation expectations.[3] Unrestricted independence allowed the Federal Reserve to finance the Great Inflation because Congress at the time

---

3 The gold standard or Bretton Woods also anchored inflationary expectations in the years prior to about 1965. This point is often neglected in the Phillips curve literature.

gave much greater concern to unemployment than to inflation. I believe Congress should restore independence but restrict Federal Reserve actions to a quasi-rule such as the Taylor Rule. If the FOMC decides to depart from the quasi-rule, it should offer both an explanation and resignations. The administration can accept the explanation or the resignations. That would better align responsibility and authority.

Some Principal Errors

Federal Reserve minutes record major errors. The Federal Reserve has never agreed on a framework for monetary policy. FOMC minutes or transcripts show many divergent views. Although the staff produces forecasts of future outcomes, the FOMC neither accepts nor rejects the staff's work. Most of the policy discussion in 1951–1986 is about near-term actions and in the 1970s and after1982 whether to change the nominal federal funds rate or reserves by one-eighth or one-quarter of a percentage point. The real rate is not mentioned. Most members did not discuss the medium or longer-term consequences of their actions. The Volcker disinflation is an exception that succeeded by concentrating on the medium-term objective of lower inflation.

In the February 14, 1972, FOMC Minutes, Sherman Maisel recognized the absence of any statement about medium-term implications: First, the FOMC did not have a clear enough picture of the relationship between changes in operating variables ... and changes in the intermediate monetary variables. Second, there was insufficient understanding of the relationship between changes in the intermediate variables and changes in the economy.... Third, there tended to be insufficient discussion of developments with respect to the demand for money.... Finally, the time period on which the Committee focused in its policy deliberations was often too short. When the Committee set its targets for intermediate variables for only a month or two ahead, it was dealing with a period in which current operations could not have much effect, and it was not taking into account the longer-run implications of its decisions [Board of Governors 1972: 5; quoted in Meltzer 2010b: 804].

Maisel's view received little support from most other members and opposition from the president of the Federal Bank of New York, Alfred Hayes, who asserted: "It had not been demonstrated that total or non-borrowed reserves had any strong or direct effects on the ultimate goals of the economy" (Board of Governors 1973: 21). His statement seems to deny any link between money and economic activity and prices, a strange position for a central banker.

Later, the FOMC set a target for some measure of reserves or money growth, but it did not permit interest rates to change enough to achieve the target. I am puzzled by these reported failures to achieve a specified target for the aggregates. The members eventually recognized that their decision to limit interest rates changes caused inflation. Yet, they kept repeating that they would not permit more interest rate variability. Their decision protected the money market from variability at the cost of failing to protect the public from inflation. Eventually, the Volcker FOMC stopped short-term interest rate control and claimed that the target was non-borrowed reserves. To avoid blame for the increase in interest rates, the market gained more freedom to change short-term interest rates. At the time, no one believed that rate would rise to 20 percent.

The staff usually explained failure to control reserves by claiming that the demand for money shifted. It never admitted that its interest rate target was inconsistent with its reserve target. When challenged occasionally by FOMC members, the staff could not support its explanation.

A repeated theme claims that the demand for money and monetary velocity are unstable. The only truth to this claim comes from overreliance on quarterly data and concentration on the immediate or near-term while ignoring longer-term effects. Figure 1 plots monetary base velocity (using the Andersen-Rasche St. Louis base) against the corporate bond rate for 78 annual observations from 1919 to 1987. The plot looks the way monetary theory says it should. There is little evidence of the alleged instability that is commonly made by members and staff.

I highlighted the years 1925 to 1928 and 1961 to 1969 to illustrate strong evidence of stability; when bond rates returned in the 1960s to the same range as in the 1920s, velocity returned to that range also. And after base velocity rose to new heights in the Great

Inflation, shown by the points at the far right, it returned along the same path during the disinflation. At annual values, Figure 1 shows considerable stability, not the instability claimed repeatedly by the Federal Reserve.

The main exception is some years of the Great Depression at the far left in Figure 1. I conclude base money velocity is a neglected indicator of medium-term policy influence and public decisions.

Figure 1
Base Velocity versus AAA Corporate Bond Rate: 1919-97

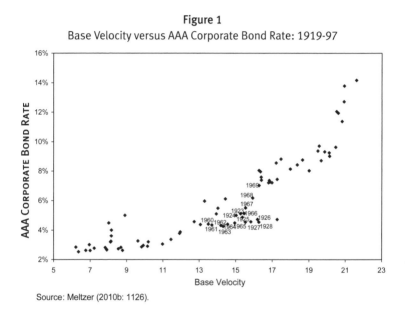

Source: Meltzer (2010b: 1126).

Why are my findings about money and velocity so different from Federal Reserve staff claims? The principal reason is that their short- term focus contrasts with my focus on the medium term. Their neglect of the medium term misleads them about the role and relevance of money growth. For every cyclical downturn from the 1920s through the 1980s, my history compares real base growth to the real long-term interest rate using the expected inflation rate instead of the actual rate after the expected rate became available. Figures 2 and 3 show two of the comparisons. In the 1953–54 cycle, real base growth falls until just before the cycle trough in May 1954, then it rises. The real interest rate falls during the decline and rises during the recovery, a pro-cyclical movement that misleads. Real base growth falls again in the months before the cyclical peak in August 1957. Real interest rates fall also. According to base growth, monetary policy tightened. Real interest rates eased.

Real base growth falls before cyclical troughs and rises before the peaks in every cycle from the 1920s to the 1980s. Real interest rates show much less consistency. The Federal Reserve never made use of this information at least in part because of its short-term focus and its neglect of the importance of money growth.

Muth (1960) developed an analysis of permanent and transitory disturbances. Economic life has many disturbances of both kinds. Some recent examples of permanent changes include the end of the Soviet Union, the Russian default, failure of Long-Term Capital, and the decline in housing prices. Neither Federal Reserve models nor the financial markets recognize that some changes persist; they are permanent changes in the environment. Existing risk models misstate risk.[4] This has created large errors at times. The Federal Reserves' near-term, short focus contributes to this error. Permanent changes appear in the "fat tails" of distributions.

The Kennedy Council of Economic Advisers introduced two major errors. First, they claimed that our market economy generated inflation before it reached full employment. The Council proposed and implemented price and wage guidelines to prevent what it considered excessive wage and price increases. No one explained, or even discussed, how control of a small subset of individual prices could prevent persistent changes in the rate of price change. This same error was central to Arthur Burns's plea for price guidelines and later President Nixon's controls. The same error reemerged in the Carter presidency. No one asked why the money the public saved because some prices were controlled would not be spent on something else, or discussed why changing a few relative prices could not prevent inflation—the rate of change of a broad index.

Proponents of guideposts and controls often claimed that corporations and labor unions exploited their monopoly power to raise prices. Burns used this reasoning repeatedly. He never explained

---

4 Brunner, Cukierman, and Meltzer (1980) develop a rational model with permanent and transitory disturbances.

Figure 2
Real Base Growth versus Real Long-Term
Interest Rate: January 1953–December 1954

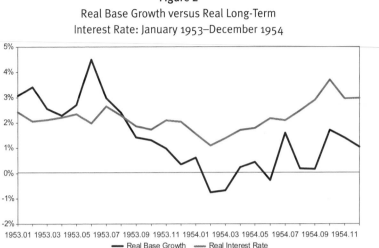

Note: Real base growth measured year-over-year; long-term interest rate measured as yield on Treasury securities with maturity greater than 10 years.

Source: Meltzer (2010a: 106).

Figure 3
RReal Base Growth versus Real Long-Term
Interest Rate: January 1955–September 1957

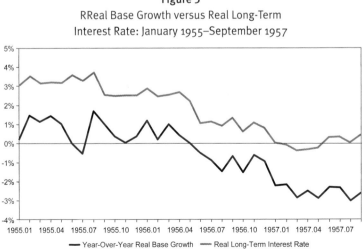

Note: Real base growth measured year-over-year; long-term interest rate measured as yield on 10-year Treasury bonds.

Source: Meltzer (2010a: 159).

why this power resulted in a *maintained* rate of price increase (inflation) and not a one-time increase in price level or a change in relative prices that exploited the monopoly power.

The confusion of price level, or relative price changes, and inflation—a maintained rate of change—was present also in the Federal Reserve's response to the oil price increases in 1973 and 1979. These were large relative price changes. Reported price index numbers rose for a time but returned to their underlying rate of increase if policy remained unchanged. Unfortunately, the Federal Reserve, at the time, did not distinguish between inflation and a relative price change, so it attempted to reverse the increase. This added to the social cost. By 2008, the Federal Reserve had learned to make the distinction, so it did not repeat the error and it began to exclude volatile relative price changes from its measure of "core inflation."

Reliance of the Phillips curve as a model of inflation was the second major problem introduced by the Kennedy Council of Economic Advisers. One error was a belief that policy could gain a permanent reduction in the unemployment rate by choosing to accept more inflation. Friedman (1968) pointed out the error. Another error that persists to the present is the use of the Phillips curve to forecast inflation. Orphanides (2001) showed that inflation forecasts persistently underestimated the inflation rate. Subsequent research established that it was a mistake to rely on available measures of the output gap because trend or full employment output varied.

Orphanides's evidence raises a question. Why did FOMC members in the 1970s rely on a forecast that persistently underestimated inflation? The answer in my history is that the politics of that period, especially during the Nixon and Carter presidencies, put greatest weight on preventing or reducing unemployment. They worried about inflation, but they mainly acted against unemployment. They used a lexicographic ordering with unemployment most important. We seem to be repeating that error now.

Policy changed in 1979 and 1980. When President Carter interviewed Paul Volcker, Volcker told him that he would act more forcefully against inflation than his predecessors had done. Carter said, "That's what I want." That was a major change. Prior to that the Carter administration was not known for an effective anti-inflation policy. It relied mainly on guideposts and exhortation. It changed, I believe, because in 1979 and 1980, opinion polls showed that the public considered inflation the most important economic problem. The public wanted to see inflation reduced, and they soon elected Ronald Reagan with a commitment to do that.

The public had not shown as much concern earlier. They changed, and the politics of controlling inflation changed with them. Chairmen of the banking committees and other members of Congress supported the Federal Reserve's efforts to reduce inflation. I believe there is an important lesson from that experience. The only successful effort to disinflate during the Great Inflation became possible only when the public opinion polls showed public support.

As early as April 1978, Vice President Mondale sent a note to President Carter to tell him that his rating on managing the economy had fallen from 47 percent to 24 percent. Mondale explained the change as a shift in public concern from unemployment to inflation. Months after appointing Volcker, President Carter yielded to congressional Democrats who urged him to use credit controls instead of high interest rates. The Federal Reserve reluctantly put on mild credit controls. The response demonstrates public concerns. Although credit cards were not controlled, many people cut their cards and mailed them to the Federal Reserve or the president. The largest quarterly fall in real GDP followed. The Federal Reserve ended credit controls in July and increased money growth. Despite urgings from his staff President Carter did not interfere with the inflation control policy again.

FOMC minutes show that two relatively successful Federal Reserve chairmen did not rely on Phillips curve forecasts. The Volcker years discussed in chapters 8 and 9 of my history contain many statements by Volcker praising the staff but remarking that their inflation forecasts were inaccurate and unreliable. In a television interview in 1980, Volcker was asked about the tradeoff between unemployment and inflation. His reply denied that the main implication of the Phillips curve was useful for policy:

> My basic philosophy is over time we have no choice but to deal with the inflationary situation because over time inflation and the unemployment go together ... Isn't that the les-

> son of the 1970s? We sat around [for] years thinking we could play off a choice between one or the other ... It had some reality when everybody thought prices were going to be stable. ... The growth situation and the employment situation will be better in an atmosphere of monetary stability than they have been in recent years [quoted in Meltzer 2010:1034].

Volcker's major policy change was to shift the weights the Federal Reserve put on inflation and unemployment by giving much more weight to reducing inflation. At first, financial markets did not show signs of belief that the change would persist once unemployment rose. Markets recalled that several prior promises to reduce inflation ended after unemployment rose. The Volcker Federal Reserve reduced skepticism by *raising* the federal funds rate when the unemployment rose to 8 percent or more in spring 1981. Expected inflation measures soon after declined.

Markets remained skeptical during the recovery. Until 1985, real rates (adjusted for expected inflation) remained from 5 to 7 percent. Investors expected inflation to return. This experience suggests one reason for the long lag between changes in money growth and its absorption into prices. Part of the lag measures the time it takes to convince the public that the Federal Reserve will persist.

Alan Greenspan also explained that he did not find the staff's Phillips curve forecasts useful. "The natural rate of unemployment, while unambiguous in a model, and useful for historical analyses, has always proved elusive when estimated in real time. The number was continually revised and did not offer a stable platform for inflation forecasting or monetary policy" (quoted in Meltzer 2010: 1034). The staff continues to rely on Phillips curve forecasts and some current members of the Board tell the public that inflation poses little danger when unemployment remains high. They neglect the fact that from 1933 to 1937 broad based price indexes rose 12 percent with unemployment rates of 17 percent or higher. And the wholesale price index rose much more.

A major cost of the greater emphasis on avoiding unemployment and reducing it when it rose was that the public learned that despite the rhetoric about commitment, the Federal Reserve would not persist in disinflation policy. Pressures from the administration, Congress, the business community, labor unions, and the public ended the commitment and the disinflation policy. Some price indexes fell to zero after a few months of disinflation in 1966. The Federal Reserve came under pressure because housing starts fell, and municipal bond yields and unemployment rose. The Federal Reserve reversed course, and inflation soon after increased.

By the early 1970s, many of the public recognized that the Federal Reserve's efforts to disinflate would be abandoned once the unemployment rate rose to 6.5 or 7 percent. Workers accepted short periods of unemployment instead of reducing wage rates. Producers accepted reduced sales instead of reducing prices. Investors demanded premiums for inflation in long-term bonds. The FOMC and others found "stagflation" puzzling. Arthur Burns and many others concluded that the pricing system no longer worked as it had. For Burns and many others, the solution was formal or informal price and wage controls. After the inflation rate fell to 2 to 3 percent in the

1980s, the problem called "stagflation" disappeared. This was an elementary set of errors. It ignored expectations based on observed policies and it failed to distinguish between price level changes and maintained rates of price change. With expected inflation low, many wages have fallen sharply during the current recession.

In the March 1960 FOMC minutes, Malcolm Bryan, president of the Federal Reserve Bank of Atlanta, urged the FOMC to control reserve growth and give more attention to the longer-term consequences of monetary actions. He pointed out that bank reserves did not increase in 1959 and fell in early 1960:

> Our policy, unless greatly ameliorated, will in a matter of time, whether weeks or months, produce effects that we do not at all want. ... Monetary policy produces lagged effects. If the effects of an overdone restriction begin sooner or later to be overtly evident, and are unfortunate, as I think they will be, we should not be able to plead ignorance. ... Let me also suggest, as a sort of aside, that the period we are in is one that illustrates the grave dangers of the free-reserve, net-borrowed reserve concept as a guide to policy" [Board of Governors 1960: 20; quoted in Meltzer 2010a: 204].

Soon after the economy was in recession. In the 1970s, Darryl Francis warned about money growth frequently. His warnings, like Bryan's, were ignored. In the 1970s, some FOMC members recognized that inflation was a monetary problem. They would not control money either because disinflation caused a temporary increase in unemployment or, more often, because monetary control required larger variation in market interest rates than they were willing to accept. The FOMC seems more concerned with protecting banks from interest rate fluctuations than in protecting the public from inflation.

Short-term market movements dominated Martin's concerns and governed his actions. He was correct that monetary economics could not predict the daily or weekly market movements that concerned him. But as Bryan and others pointed out at times, inflation would not be controlled using his procedures. Although Martin opposed inflation and made many speeches warning about the consequences of sustained inflation, the inflation rate reached 6 percent in 1970, the last year of his service.

One of the persistent errors was a consequence of the money market focus. Free reserves—member bank excess reserves minus borrowing—rose when borrowing declined and fell when borrowing increased. The decline in bank borrowing and in loan demand lowered other interest rates and money growth. A rise in bank borrowing had the opposite effect; the monetary base, money, and interest rates rose.

The Federal Reserve interpreted the fall in free reserves and the rise in interest rates as contractionary. Monetarists claimed that the increase in the monetary base and money showed that monetary pol- icy was expansive. This difference in interpretation persisted. The movements of base velocity shown earlier support the monetarist interpretation of events.

One consequence was that money growth rose during economic expansions and fell during economic contractions. Federal Reserve policy was pro-cyclical. It prolonged recessions and increased inflations. Monetarists repeated their criticism frequently, but the Federal Reserve retained its interpretation.

Fed Governor Sherman Maisel pointed out in 1970 that when he became a member of the Board, he received hundreds of pages of material. None explained how the Federal Reserve made decisions. There was no written record and no agreement among the participants. More surprising to me is that there was never a discussion of the principles guiding monetary policy and no effort to agree on a broad framework. In fact, the Martin FOMC did not use forecasts until the mid-1960s. The "Riefler rule" forbade forecasting.

Later, the Board's staff developed an econometric model and several Reserve banks also had models. FOMC members received fore- casts in advance of each meeting, but the minutes suggest that members did not rely on or agree to the staff forecast and, as mentioned earlier, Paul Volcker and Alan Greenspan did not find the staffs' forecasts useful.

Let me mention a few additional errors that appear frequently. The minutes rarely distinguish between real and nominal exchange rates and real and nominal interest rates. Members considered an 8 percent federal funds rate high even as inflation rose to 8 percent. The forecasting staff prepared forecasts without any consideration of monetary policy. James Pierce, a deputy research director pointed that out, but procedures did not change. The FOMC followed an "even keel" policy of holding nominal interest rates unchanged for weeks surrounding a Treasury financing. By the late 1960s, this policy severely restricted the time available for policy operations. Reserves supplied during even keel were not withdrawn, so they contributed to inflation.

There were other errors as well. The Federal Reserve was reluctant to urge the Treasury to auction securities, so it continued to sup- port bond sales by increasing reserves, and the staff estimated the volume of reserves released or absorbed by changes in reserve requirement ratios. It failed to recognize that with interest rates unchanged, total reserves would not change.

After Congress passed Resolution 133 and later the Humphrey-Hawkins Act, the FOMC issued projections of rates of growth of several monetary aggregates. Actual growth often exceeded the projection. Instead of adjusting the next projection, the Committee based the next projection on the existing level. Several members, perhaps influenced by a staff study by Bill Poole, noted that this procedure gave an inflationary bias to the monetary aggregates, but the FOMC did not change.

Brief Summary of 1951–86 Actions

In the book, the history of the years 1951–86 covers nearly 1,400 pages. All that I can do here is discuss a few highlights. I concentrate on inflation.

The main monetary policy events of the 1950s were the March1951 Accord with the Treasury that permitted the Federal Reserve to raise the rates on long-term bonds above the 2.5 percent ceiling established in 1942 to help finance World War II. As part of the Accord, the Federal Reserve agreed to assist the Treasury in financing the debt. This was the reason for even-keel policy. It became a reason for inflationary policy.

The new chairman, William McChesney Martin, Jr., negotiated the agreement for the Treasury. Martin had experience in financial markets. He was skeptical about the value of economics for monetary policy, and he claimed that he did not understand the money supply. I conclude that the reason was the extremely short-run focus on the money market reflected in his use of free reserves or color, tone, and feel as main indicators. This usage hid the medium- and long-term consequences of his policy until inflation arrived.

Nevertheless, Martin maintained relatively low inflation in the 1950s. A main reason was that Presidents Truman and Eisenhower avoided large budget deficits except in recessions. President Truman raised tax rates to finance the Korean War, and the Eisenhower administration ran budget surpluses in several years. By 1960, when President Eisenhower left office, the actual and expected inflation rate was about zero.

The Eisenhower administration began a series of meetings with the Federal Reserve chairman that later became known as the Quadriad. During the Kennedy administration and even more force- fully under President Johnson, the administration attempted to restrict Federal Reserve independence by promoting "policy coordination." Many academic economists favored coordination. In practice, it meant that the Federal Reserve would finance budget deficits. When the time came to reduce the budget deficit, coordination did not work. Even worse, administration economists and the Board staff predicted "fiscal overkill" once the 1968 tax surcharge became law. They urged the FOMC to ease monetary policy. By year-end Chairman Martin knew that he had made a mistake by responding to the pressures for easier monetary policy. Inflation rose. The inflation problem increased because people expected inflation to continue. Policy actions to end disinflation policy in 1967 and in 1970 when unemployment rose strengthened inflation expectations. Later experience reinforced the belief that inflation had lower priority than unemployment.

Deficit finance to pay for the Vietnam War and the Great Society and policy coordination were main reasons that the Great Inflation started. They were not the only reasons. The Kennedy Council of Economic Advisers believed it was socially desirable to increase inflation to lower unemployment. They gave no role to expected inflation. Instead, they claimed that they could use guideposts and guidelines to control price movements. This argument confused control of the level of a few relative prices and some money wages with control of the maintained rate of price change. Proponents never considered why successful control of some relative prices would control aggregate spending if money growth remained unchanged.

Mentioning the Council of Economic Advisers brings attention to the role taken by academic economists. The dominant view in the academic profession at the time was based on a simple Keynesian model such as the model in Ackley (1961). Economists could change outcomes by changing taxes and government spending. Monetary policy had the task of controlling interest rates to permit the economy to realize the full effect of fiscal policy. Expectations or crowding out did not appear. During the 1960s, Ackley was chairman of the president's council.

Dissent from these views was heard at the time, but did not influence policy until much later. Arthur Okun, the last chairman of President Johnson's council, dismissed Milton Friedman's (1968) presidential address as theoretically correct but practically irrelevant. He expected inflation to decline along the same Phillips curve on which it rose. He recognized later that that didn't happen.

The economists on President Nixon's Council of Economic Advisers accepted Friedman's analysis and believed that excessive money growth was the principal cause of inflation. However, they responded to political pressures to reduce the unemployment rate first and reduce inflation later. Most often, they urged the Federal Reserve to increase money growth.

President Kennedy expressed concern about the loss of gold and, at one point, threatened to take U.S. troops out of Europe to stop French and German gold purchases. French President deGaulle believed it was an empty threat. France continued to buy gold from the U.S. stock. Germany stopped.

The Johnson administration used controls to prevent payments crises from spreading. By 1968, only governments and central banks could buy gold from the U.S. stock, and they were discouraged from buying. By the end of Martin's term in 1970, inflation reached 6 percent and the Bretton Woods system of fixed exchange rates was close to its end.

The administration and the Federal Reserve participated in numerous meetings in the 1960s to create Special Drawing Rights (SDRs). They gave no attention to exchange rate adjustment. Critics pointed out the mistake; the authorities ignored the criticisms.

In February 1970, Arthur Burns replaced Martin as chairman. Burns had publicly criticized the use of guideposts by the Kennedy and Johnson administrations, but shortly after becoming Federal Reserve chairman he became a principal advocate. Burns never clearly distinguished price level changes from change in the rate of price change. He blamed inflation on labor unions, monopolies, and the welfare state. Of course, he heard about money growth from his friend Milton Friedman, but he rejected Friedman's warnings. After he left office, he recognized that money growth was the principal cause of inflation but he explained that central bankers could not reduce money growth because of social pressures from labor unions, monopolies, etc.

Burns served two terms as chairman. He wanted reappointment, but the Carter administration wanted a more cooperative and congenial chairman. They chose William Miller. Miller negotiated the end of Regulation Q. He did not act effectively against inflation. After about 18 months, he left to become secretary of the Treasury.

Paul Volcker came next. President Carter appointed a known anti-inflationist. The president had not shown much interest in monetary control earlier, but he seems to have learned that guideposts, in any of his administration's adumbrations, would not control inflation. With the election approaching, and the public telling pollsters that the inflation was the country's main economic problem, President Carter accepted Paul Volcker's statement that he would be more active against inflation than his predecessors.

Volcker took office in August 1979. In September, the Board raised the discount rate on a 4 to 3 vote. Volcker thought the market would interpret the increase as evidence of his intentions. Instead, many read the 4 to 3 vote as a sign of dissension and weakness. Volcker learned that incremental changes were not likely to work.

In early October, the FOMC unanimously agreed to control growth of bank reserves. The decision reduced the FOMC's responsibility for the rise in interest rates. In practice, they restricted changes in interest rates at times, but they did not prevent the funds rates from reaching 20 percent.

Reserve control was imperfect and erratic at times. Banks borrowed reserves at rates often far below the federal funds rate. Control imperfections may have prolonged the disinflationary period. Three other changes worked to make the anti-inflation policy succeed.

First, Volcker got the FOMC to make inflation control its priority. He reversed the lexicographic ordering by putting inflation control first. Several earlier efforts failed, despite strong statements by FOMC members, because the FOMC abandoned anti-inflation actions when the unemployment rate rose. Many believed the same would happen after 1979. Their beliefs received support when the Federal Reserve adopted credit controls and increased money growth in the spring of 1980.

Second, the Volcker Fed began to change expectations when it raised interest rates in April 1981 with the unemployment rate about

8 percent. Contrary to several Keynesian forecasts made during the period, the expected rate of inflation fell quickly. Within less than 18 months, annual rates of inflation fell to 3 or 4 percent. The unemployment rate rose above 10.5 percent.

International and domestic financial failures brought "practical monetarism" to an end. Money growth increased and the economy recovered. Economic research has not given much attention to the fact that recovery occurred in 1983 and real growth rose despite real long-term interest rates as high as 7 percent. Real rates remained high for several years. Markets seem to have expected inflation to return in the mid-1980s. When that didn't happen, expected inflation and long-term rates declined.

My book ends with the end of expected inflation. I chose 1985–86 as that date because, at last, money wages, exchange rates, and long- term interest rates had settled at rates that did not anticipate a return of high inflation. Figure 4 shows the decline in money wage growth after 1981. By 1984, wage growth reached a noninflationary rate. This is the start of the period described as the "Great Moderation."

Money growth and inflation were moderate. Long expansions ended in mild recessions. Per capita real disposable income increased 50 percent from 1986 to 2005. Complaints shifted from aggregate to distributional results. Unemployment and inflation remained broadly consistent with a Taylor Rule.

Figure 4
Quarterly Change in Nominal Compensation per Hour:
Four-Quarter Moving Average, 1971–90

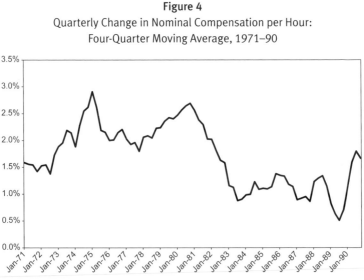

Source: Meltzer (2010b: 1167).

Misperceptions and Mistakes

As I noted near the start, most of the errors that I find in Federal Reserve policy are found in the minutes. Members of FOMC urged changes to avoid major problems. Most comments of this kind received no response, and changes did not follow.

The models or frameworks used to analyze events made a major contribution to policy mistakes. The simple Keynesian theory in the 1960s replaced the real bills doctrine from the 1920s and 1930s as a source of error. Neglect of expectations and efforts to permanently reduce the unemployment rate by increasing inflation reinforced the mistakes.

The chairmen and members of FOMC did not slavishly follow an economic model. Many regarded themselves as practical people, making judgments based on what they saw and heard. This was especially true of Chairman Martin in the 1950s. He did not find economics useful, especially the economics of money.

Martin was not alone. With the exception of the Volcker disinflation, money growth is dismissed as irrelevant. I believe the reason

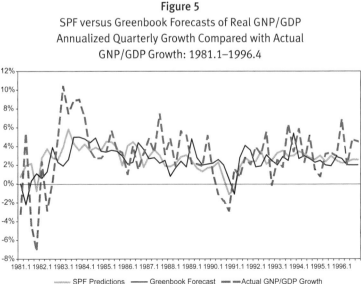

Figure 5
SPF versus Greenbook Forecasts of Real GNP/GDP
Annualized Quarterly Growth Compared with Actual
GNP/GDP Growth: 1981.1–1996.4

Source: Meltzer (2010a: 1140).

Figure 6
SPF versus Greenbook Forecasts of GNP/GDP
Implicit Price Deflator Annualized Quarterly Growth Compared
with Actual Deflator Growth: 1971.4–1980.4

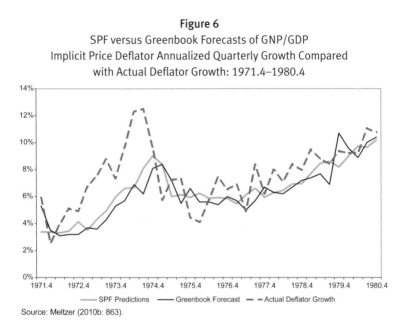

Source: Meltzer (2010b: 863).

mainly reflects another failing—excessive attention to near-term actual or perhaps expected events and the neglect of longer-term implications of policy actions. The minutes that I read through 1986 contain numerous pages discussing whether the FOMC should change the funds rate by one-eighth or one-quarter of 1 percent, but there was nothing or almost nothing about longer-term consequences. Volcker freed the FOMC from this type of myopia for only three years. It returned.

Figures 5 and 6 compare market consensus projections of growth and inflation to Federal Reserve forecasts and actual growth rates. The periods shown differ, but for both charts the large errors are forecast errors not data revision errors. One disconcerting finding is the persistent large difference between actual inflation and inflation forecasts from 1971 to 1974. The same problem reappears from 1976 to 1979. The forecasts underestimated inflation almost all the time.

Orphanides (1981) showed that inaccurate Phillips curve forecasts were a major reason for the error.

Figure 7
Median Forecast of Real Output from Survey of Professional
Forecasters versus "Real-Time" Real Output: 1971.1–1999.3

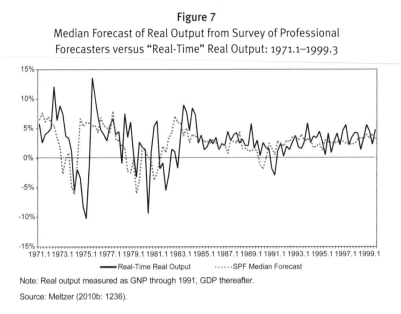

Note: Real output measured as GNP through 1991, GDP thereafter.

Source: Meltzer (2010b: 1236).

Members of FOMC knew about the forecast errors. Paul Volcker
and Alan Greenspan did not rely on Phillips curve forecasts. Both
chairmen praised the staff but disregarded the forecasts, regarding
them as inaccurate. Both recognized that, contrary to the Phillips
curve, on average inflation and unemployment rates were positively
related in the 1970s and 1980s.

Figure 5 suggests that forecast errors for real GDP are often
large, often much larger than differences between Federal Reserve
and market consensus forecasts. Figure 7 shows forecast errors for
real GDP growth from 1971 to 1999. Large errors and persistent errors show how difficult it is to forecast quarterly changes.

The puzzle is that the Federal Reserve gives so much attention
to the near-term and so little to longer-term consequences. They
know, as we all should know, that economics is not the science that
gives accurate near-term forecasts of inflation and output growth.
There is no such science. Further, even if near-term forecasts improved greatly there is good reason to believe that policy changes
would not have much near-term effect.

A related part of the puzzle is that policy can have a predictable effect on medium-term inflation. Several countries have adopted inflation targets that aim at inflation 2 or 3 years ahead. The U.S. Congress has not accepted an inflation target, and the Federal Reserve has not adopted one.

The Future

Currently, the Federal Reserve faces two major problems. The government has announced that it plans $9 trillion dollars of budget deficits over the next decade. They do not tell us how they propose to finance the deficits or how they might reduce them. The Federal Reserve increased bank reserves by more than $1 trillion, from $800 billion to $2.2 trillion after the Lehman failure in 2008. At the time I write measured excess reserves are $1 trillion. It is disingenuous and wrong to tell the public that most of the problem will be handled by paying interest on bank reserves or selling non-marketable securities. How high do they believe the interest rate must rise to get banks to hold hundreds of billions of reserves after loan demand increases? And does the staff model recognize that banks see the lending rate, not the funds rate, as the relevant opportunity cost? To plan for the future, the public should be told how these enormous deficits will be financed and how excess reserves will be reduced. History does not record any example of countries that faced high money growth, large and growing budget deficits, and a depreciating currency that escaped inflation. The only examples to the contrary are countries that adopted strong disinflationary fiscal and monetary policies. The United States has not begun to make the changes that will be needed. This is another example of lexicographic ordering and a short-term focus.

My history shows that the meaning of Federal Reserve independence changed several times after 1951. Paul Volcker restored independence after the Great Inflation. Much of that independence was surrendered in the recent crisis.

History suggests that independence and public support of disinflation will be critical in reducing reserves to prevent inflation. During the 1970s the FOMC determined to reduce inflation several times. It did not persist. As unemployment and interest rates rose, voices in Congress, the administration, business, labor, and the public called for lower interest rates, higher growth, and more employment. Policy changed.

The Volcker disinflation had public support. Opinion polls showed inflation as the public's most serious problem. The public elected Ronald Reagan on a program to reduce inflation and restore growth. And leading members of Congress, including chair- men of the banking committees, supported a disinflation policy. Those conditions are not present at current and prospective rates of inflation.

What should the Federal Reserve do? They should announce the details of their plan and explain the plan and its likely consequences to the Congress and the public.

Congress should accept and endorse an independent Federal Reserve, but in return the Fed should accept restrictions on its actions. Central bank independence began under the gold standard. Central banks received protection from financing the government but agreed to abide by gold standard rules. After the gold standard ended, that restriction no longer limited discretion. One consequence is that the Federal Reserve can increase unemployment and inflation. The public cannot sanction the Fed. It blames its political representatives.

Back in 1980, I proposed that the Federal Reserve should announce its planned growth and inflation targets. If it misses the target by more than a minor error, it should offer an explanation and a resignation. The president can accept the explanation or the resignation. That closes some of the gap between authority and responsibility.

After the New Zealand central bank heard my proposal, they improved on it by choosing the inflation target in negotiation with the government. Many other governments followed. The United States has not.

Another reform requires recognition of the failure to announce a rule for lender-of-last-resort. In 96 years, the Federal Reserve has not adopted a rule of this type. This increases uncertainty as comparison of the response to Lehman and AIG shows. Who knew what would happen next? Also, absence of a rule encourages failing firms to pressure Congress to pressure the Federal Reserve. And, bailouts induce risk taking and moral hazard.

The Federal Reserve and Congress should agree on a lender-of-last-resort rule. Bagehot's rule from 19th century Britain is an excel- lent starting point. When the Bank of England followed the rule, there were failures, but failures did not end in crisis. Banks borrowed against good collateral.

The lender-of-last-resort rule should be part of a reform that includes ending the "too big to fail" policy of the past 30 years. That policy promotes gigantism, moral hazard, and encourages excessive risk. The policy protects large banks at public expense. And it distorts markets by supporting large banks while letting smaller banks fail. A correct policy would protect the public not the large banks.

To implement the policy, Congress should require that, beyond some moderate size, banks must increase capital more than in pro- portion to their increase in asset size. To prevent failures from spreading to counterparties, banks should have a right to borrow from the Fed on acceptable collateral. Gains from economies of scale and scope do not compensate the public for losses from bailouts. And banks that receive aid should be required to repay, as Chile requires.

Many critics of economics claim that economists failed to forecast the housing and financial crisis. This criticism assumes that economics is the science that provides accurate forecasts. For 50 years, some of us showed that near-term events can be approximated as a random walk.

Forecasts can be improved, however. Muth (1960) showed how to analyze permanent or persistent errors. Few if any financial institutions use Muth's procedure. The Board of Governors model does not admit persistent shocks, or permanent changes in the environment. The Russian default, housing price declines, failure of Long-Term Capital, and many other persistent changes produced major market disturbances. We cannot expect to predict permanent changes, but we can improve the ability to recognize them when they occur.

Finally, I repeat my earlier proposal to increase both price and exchange rate stability. We know that no country acting alone can provide both, but both are desirable. My proposal calls for agreement by the major currency providers—the United States, the European Central Bank, Japan, and China (if it develops a less restricted monetary system). The countries would agree to maintain inflation between

0 and 2 percent. Any country that fixed its currency to the low inflation currencies would import low inflation and maintain a fixed exchange rate. The United States, Japan, and the ECB would benefit from fixed exchange rates and low inflation in countries that fix. Countries that chose to float their currency could do so, but they would lose the public benefit. Real exchange rates would remain flexible.

Conclusion

In its 96 year history, the Federal Reserve has adapted to extraordinary changes in political and monetary arrangements. Its record, however, is not without failures and errors.

Reforms should be made, to reduce errors. Discretion should be limited by a rule or quasi-rule, preferably one that is compatible with low inflation policies abroad. Congress and the Federal Reserve should agree on a rule for the lender-of-last-resort and follow it.

The most important single change in policymaking would change the FOMC's focus from very-near-term events to increased attention to longer-term consequences of its actions. In its long history, there are few periods of sustained growth and low inflation. The years of the Great Moderation are an exception. At that time, the Federal Reserve acted as if it followed a Taylor Rule. More attention to longer-term consequences embedded in a quasi-rule like the Taylor Rule is a start. Once the FOMC abandons excessive attention to near-term events, it will find that money growth is an imperfect but useful guide on which to rely.

Through most of its history, the Federal Reserve followed lexicographic ordering with unemployment its principal concern. When it shifted concern to inflation, unemployment rose. Concern shifted back to unemployment. In 1980–82, disinflation was its main concern. Currently, it is back to concentrating on reducing the unemployment rate. Instead of following its dual mandate, it takes one objective at a time. The result in the 1970s was that both unemployment and inflation rose on average. And in the 1980s both declined.

The Fed's massive intervention to rescue the large banks and respond to rising unemployment is not matched by an effective strategy to prevent inflation. Although Chairman Bernanke told us repeatedly that excess reserves would decline when banks and others repaid their short-term debt, it didn't happen. Instead the Fed increased mortgage holdings. These actions introduce large amounts of long-term, illiquid assets onto the Fed's balance sheet. Nothing like this has ever occurred. It abrogates independence by allocating credit to help the housing industry and by mixing credit policy and monetary policy. Also, it makes it more difficult to reduce the massive volume of excess reserves. Who will buy the massive holding of illiquid mortgages?

Classical economists understood that when real cash balances rise above the public's desired holdings, the public buys assets and/or output. When real balances fall below desired levels, the public accumulates balances and prices fall until desired real balances are reached. The annual demand for base money and money is sufficiently stable to make this classical or neoclassical proposition useful, more useful I expect that many of the propositions that are in vogue.

Most of the economic models used in the academic literature and at the Federal Reserve do not include asset prices and credit markets. One exception that reflects the emphasis on asset markets as well as output and prices is in the series of papers that I did with Karl Brunner.[5] This work analyzes the interaction of money, debt, and capital markets as the process that characterizes the credit and money markets. How can a central bank analyze or regulate banks and financial institutions correctly using models limited to output markets in which money has no role?

Finally, the recurring issue of the role of Federal Reserve bank presidents is again active. In the past Congress has not changed their role. That is the right decision, I believe. It retains the broad influence brought by the presidents, representing regional as well

---

5   Brunner and Meltzer (1993) summarize this work, much of which is available also in major journals.

as national interests. In the past, the regional banks have proposed important changes. St. Louis pressed for the increased attention to money, real interest rates, and inflation that became Fed policy from 1979 to 1982. Minneapolis has led in the effort to reform the response to bank failures, and all regional banks bring information from business, labor, and consumers. Moreover, the regional banks are less influenced by political pressures. This valuable role is the heart of President Wilson's compromise that created the Federal Reserve. The compromise should be retained.

References

Ackley, G. (1961) *Macroeconomic Theory*. New York: Macmillan. Board of Governors of the Federal Reserve System (various dates)

Minutes of the Federal Open Market Committee.
Washington: Federal Reserve System (unpublished).

Brunner, K.; Cukierman, A.; and Meltzer, A. H. (1980) "Stagflation, Persistent Unemployment, and the Permanence of Economic Shocks." *Journal of Monetary Economics* 6 (October): 467–92.

Brunner, K. and Meltzer, A. H. (1993) *Money and the Economy: Issues in Monetary Analysis.* The Raffaele Mattioli Lectures. Cambridge: Cambridge University Press.

Burns, A. F. ([1979] 1987) "The Anguish of Central Banking."
Federal Reserve Bulletin (September): 687–98.

Friedman, M. (1968) "The Role of Monetary Policy."
American Economic Review 58 (March): 1–17.

Meltzer, A. H. (2003) *A History of the Federal Reserve, Volume 1, 1913–1951.* Chicago: University of Chicago Press.

_____(2010a) *A History of the Federal Reserve, Volume 2, Book 1, 1951–1969.* Chicago: University of Chicago Press.

_____(2010b) *A History of the Federal Reserve, Volume 2, Book 2, 1970–1986.* Chicago: University of Chicago Press.

Muth, J. F. (1960) "Optimal Properties of Exponentially Weighted Forecasts."
Journal of the American Statistical Association 55 (June): 299–306.

Orphanides, A. (2001) "Monetary Policy Rules Based on Real-Time Data."
American Economic Review 91 (September): 964–85.

L Street: Bagehotian Prescriptions for a 21st Century Money Market

George Selgin[1]

In *Lombard Street*, Walter Bagehot (1873) offered his famous advice for reforming the Bank of England's lending policy. The financial crisis of 1866, and other factors, had convinced Bagehot that instead of curtailing credit to conserve the Bank's own liquidity in the face of an "internal drain" of specie, and thereby confronting the English economy as a whole with a liquidity shortage, the Bank ought to "lend freely at high rates on good collateral." Bagehot's now-famous advice has come to be known as the "classical" prescription for last-resort lending.

Largely forgotten, however, is Bagehot's belief that his prescription was but a second-best remedy for financial crises, far removed from the first-best remedy, namely, the substitution of a decentralized banking system—such as Scotland's famously stable free banking system—for England's centralized arrangement. Bagehot's excuse for proffering such a remedy was simply that he did not think anyone was prepared to administer the first-best alternative: "I propose to maintain this system," he wrote, "because I am quite sure it is of no manner of use proposing to alter it. . . . You might as well, or better, try to alter the English monarchy and substitute a republic" (Bagehot 1873: 329–30).

Like Bagehot, I offer here some second-best suggestions, informed by recent experience, for improving existing arrangements for dealing with financial crises. Unlike Bagehot, who merely recommended changes in the Bank of England's *conduct*, I propose changes to the Federal Reserve's *operating framework*. And although, like Bagehot, I consider my proposals mere "palliatives," I do not assume that we cannot ultimately do better: on the contrary, I doubt that any amount of mere tinkering with our existing, discretionary central banking system will suffice to protect us against future financial crises. To truly reduce the risk of such crises, we must

---

1 *Cato Journal*, Vol. 32, No. 2 (Spring/Summer 2012).

seriously consider more radical reforms (see, e.g., Selgin, Lastrapes, and White 2010).

A Top-Heavy Operating System

Both the financial crisis and the ways in which the Fed felt compelled to respond to it point to shortcomings of the Fed's traditional operating framework—a framework that relies heavily on a small number of systematically important financial firms known as "primary dealers," as well as on JPMorgan and Bank of New York Mellon in their capacity as "clearing banks" for the Fed's temporary open market transactions.

In theory these private institutions serve as efficient monetary policy agents—that is, as private middlemen or conduits through which liquidity is supplied by the Fed to the rest of the financial system. The theory breaks down, however, if the agents themselves become illiquid or insolvent, or if some agents fear being damaged by the liquidity or insolvency of others. In that case, the agents may cease to be effective monetary policy conduits. Instead, their involvement can undermine the implementation of ordinary monetary pol- icy, denying solvent firms access to liquid assets. The Fed may for these reasons alone—and setting aside others that contribute to the agents' "systematic significance"—be compelled to bail out a monetary policy agent, further interfering with efficient credit allocation. The expectation that it will do so in turn enhances agents' "too big to fail" status, encouraging them to take excessive risks, and increasing the likelihood of future crises.

In what follows I explore the drawbacks of the Fed's top-heavy operating framework, especially as revealed by the recent financial crisis. I then offer suggestions for making that framework both less top-heavy and more flexible. The suggested reforms should serve to reduce both the extent of the Fed's interference with an efficient allocation of credit and the extent of implicit guarantees in the financial system, while making it easier for the Fed to adhere to the spirit of Bagehot's classical rules for last-resort lending. More specifically, the changes I recommend seek to ground Fed operations more firmly in the rule of law—and make them less subject to the rule of men—by allowing the Fed to rely on one and the same operating framework to both implement normal monetary policy and meet extraordinary liquidity needs during times of financial distress.

Ordinary Monetary Operations

The Fed traditionally conducts monetary policy by means of a combination of "permanent" and "temporary" open market operations. Permanent operations involve outright purchases and sales of Treasury securities. Because permanent open market sales are relatively rare, purchased securities are usually held in the Fed's System Open Market Account (SOMA) until they mature. Permanent open market purchases are mainly used to provide for secular growth in the stock of base money, and especially in the outstanding stock of paper currency.

Temporary open market operations, in contrast, are aimed at making seasonal and cyclical adjustments to the stock of base money, and are typically conducted, not by means of outright purchases and sales of Treasury securities, but by means of repurchase agreements or "repos" involving such securities. Although in name a repo is contract providing for the sale of a security with an agreement by the seller to repurchase the same security at a specified price within a relatively short period after the initial sale, in practice repos resemble collateralized loans in which the security to be repurchased serves as collateral. The Fed, having first introduced repos to the U.S. economy in 1917, shied away from them after the massive bank failures of the 1930s. They came back into favor as monetary policy instruments following the 1951 Treasury Accord. Eventually a private repo market developed in which repos, instead of being confined to Treasury securities, came to include a broad range of private debt instruments (Acharya and Öncü 2010: 323–30).

The self-reversing nature of repos, and the fact that the vast majority of them are overnight loans, make them especially fit for temporary open market operations, because the Fed has only to refrain from renewing its repos to absorb base money after a peak demand for it subsides. Repos come in handy, for example, during the Christmas season, when the Fed uses them to offset the decline in bank reserves that must otherwise result from heavy currency withdrawals. Repos also help the Fed to implement its federal funds rate target, because for banks overnight Treasury repos are a relatively close substitute for borrowing in the federal funds market. Arbitrage thus tends to cause the federal funds rate to track the rate for such repos. The Fed is consequently able to use repos to move the federal funds rate in whatever direction it desires, and move it more assuredly than it could do using outright Treasury purchases and sales.

Both permanent and temporary open market operations have traditionally been conducted with a limited number of counterparties known as primary dealers. Although the roots of this primary dealer system trace to 1935, when the Fed was first prevented from buying bonds directly from the U.S. Treasury, the system officially got started with 18 members in 1960. By 1988 the number had climbed to 46. But on the eve of the crisis it had dwindled to just 20, including a dozen foreign bank affiliates. Today, after the failure of MF Global—one of two post-crisis additions to the list—there are 21. The Fed normally conducts its open market operations with these dealers only, arranging both outright Treasury security purchases and repos with them, and leaving it to them to channel funds to other financial firms mainly by means of private repos, with commercial banks in turn sharing reserves through the overnight federal funds market.

Two other private market agents also assist the Fed in implementing monetary policy. The failure of two major security dealers during the 1980s gave rise to so-called "tri-party" repos, in which repo counterparties, including the Fed, rely on third parties, known as clearing banks, to price and otherwise manage repo collateral. Today, as at the time of the crisis, there are only two such banks— JPMorgan Chase and the Bank of New York Mellon. Besides being conduits for the Fed's open market operations, the clearing banks also play a crucial role in allocating available liquidity among primary dealers.

Ordinarily, as Donald Kohn (2009: 6) observes, the primary dealer system "allows the Federal Reserve to implement policy quite efficiently . . .with minimal interference in private credit markets." Because it relies on the private market to price and direct funds, the system avoids any risk of credit being provided at subsidized rates, and so heeds Bagehot's classical prescription. The Fed nevertheless maintains a standing facility—the discount window— for the purpose of direct lending to illiquid financial institutions, partly in recognition of the possibility that open market operations, as ordinarily conducted, may prove inadequate for meeting "serious financial strains among individual firms or specialized groups of institutions" during times of financial distress (Board of Governors 1971: 19).

Generally speaking, the presence of efficient wholesale lending markets means that banks are unlikely to turn to the discount window unless they lack the sort of good collateral that would qualify them for classical last-resort loans. The Fed, for its part, appears unable to resist lending to insolvent banks.[2] Consequently, several economists (Friedman 1960: 50–51 and 1982; Humphrey 1986; Goodfriend and King 1988; Kaufman 1991, 1999; Lacker 2004:

956ff.; and Hetzel 2009) have recommended doing away with extended discount-window lending altogether, and having the Fed supply liquidity solely through the open market. The crisis has, how- ever, been regarded by some as proof that such a step would be imprudent. "A systemic event," Stephen Checchetti and Titi Disyata (2010: 12) observe, "almost surely requires lending at an effectively subsidized rate" secured by "collateral of suspect quality," which can be had only by direct appeal to a central bank.

Further consideration suggests, however, that the apparent need for direct lending during crises stems, not from the inadequacy of open market operations as such, but from the inadequacy of the Fed's particular rules and procedures for conducting such operations, including its reliance upon the primary dealer system.[3]

In particular the Fed, by depending upon a small set of primary dealers, and on two clearing banks, for its open market operations,

---

2 According to a Congressional study of discount window lending during the late 1980s, of 418 banks that received discount window loans, nearly all had CAMEL scores of 5, indicating effective insolvency, at the time; and about 90 percent of them subsequently failed (Kaufman 1999:4; see also Schwartz 1992).

3 Even considered with regard to the Fed's traditional open market procedures Checchetti and Disyata's claim appears too strong: open market operations have sufficed to preserve market liquidity during several past "systemic events," including the failure of Penn Central, the October 1987 stock market crash, Y2K, and 9/11.

risks a breakdown in the monetary transmission mechanism when these agents themselves become troubled. Consequently the Fed may be compelled, not merely to engage in direct lending, but also to depart from Bagehot's principles by bailing out insolvent firms when their failure threatens to cause a breakdown in its operating framework. The Fed's reliance upon primary dealers and tri-party repos thus contributes to the notion of the "systemically important financial institution" (SIFI), official recognition of which, according to former Kansas City Fed President Thomas Hoenig (2011), poses a serious threat to the future of capitalism.

While some firms would perhaps continue to be regarded as "systematically important" no matter how monetary policy is conducted, a responsible central bank ought to avoid arrangements that contribute to the existence of such financial goliaths, to the extent that it can do so without otherwise compromising its ability to conduct monetary policy. Policymakers should in turn welcome new arrangements that might do away with a perceived need for ad hoc changes to the Fed's operating procedures in response to systemic events.

Monetary Operations during the Subprime Crisis

The Fed's primary dealer-based operating system takes primary dealers' financial health for granted. If the dealers themselves are in danger of failing, the system can break down.

Primary dealers are hardly likely to go broke owing to their participation in open market operations. However, the set of primary dealers "overlaps substantially" with that of major dealers in securities and OTC derivatives, and such dealers "tend to finance significant fractions of their assets with short-term repurchase agreements" with counterparties consisting mainly of other dealers, money market mutual funds, and securities lenders (Duffie 2009: 9, 27–8). Hence, dealers' notoriously high leverage. When a dealer's solvency becomes suspect, its counterparties may choose not to renew their repos with it, so as to avoid risks involved in having to realize on their collateral. The general refusal of a dealer's counterparties to renew can force the dealer into bankruptcy, while its attempts to provide for its own liquidity at short notice could threaten other dealers by contributing to a general decline in the market value of, and hence an increase in haircuts applied to, private security repos.

An increased perceived risk of primary dealer insolvency can short-circuit monetary policy in at least two ways. First, as just noted, an increase in perceived counterparty risk may cause prospective private lenders to cease lending to them except perhaps at very high rates. Second, highly leveraged banks, including dealers, upon realizing that adverse asset shocks have increased their own debt rollover risk, may "hoard" liquidity by refraining from lending—and especially from term lending—even to counterparties that they know to be solvent (Acharya and Skeie 2011). Consequently, instead of serving as efficient conduits for the transmission of reserves, dealers become so many liquidity traps, contributing to the drying-up of wholesale lending markets. The drying-up of liquidity in turn con- tributes to the perceived riskiness of nondealer counterparties, and hence to more liquidity hoarding, possibly leading to a general credit freeze.

Such a freeze appears to have hampered monetary policy during the subprime crisis when, as various Federal Reserve officials have themselves acknowledged, instead of assisting the Fed in keeping financial markets liquid, the primary dealer system "blocked, or seriously undermined, the mechanisms through which monetary policy influences the economy" (Fisher and Rosenblum 2009; cf. Afonso, Kovner, and Schoar 2011). At the onset of the crisis, during the third quarter of 2007, primary dealers, having been among the financial institutions faced with the largest toxic asset losses, were also "the quickest to freeze or reduce their lending activity" (Fisher and Rosenblum 2009), and so ceased to be a source of liquidity to either businesses or to other banks (Giles and Tett 2008). According to Kohn (2009: 6),

The fact that primary dealers rather than commercial banks were the regular counterparties of the Federal Reserve in its open market operations, together with the fact that the Federal Reserve ordinarily extended only modest amounts of funding through repo agreements, meant that open market operations were not particularly useful during the crisis for directing funding to where it was most critically needed in the financial system.

In consequence, and despite the Fed's considerable lowering of its federal funds rate target, interest rates paid by business and households rose. Sound banks that, thanks to the reduced volume of wholesale lending, found themselves short of liquidity, had the option of turning to the Fed's discount window, but refrained from doing so owing to the stigma associated with discount window borrowing ever since the Fed's 1984 bailout of Continental Illinois. It was thanks to this credit "distribution bottleneck" that the Fed was driven to create "an array of mechanisms by which institutions, other than primary dealers, could properly avail of official liquidity provision" (Dunne, Fleming, and Zholos 2009: 4), including the Term Auction Facility (TAF)—a term repo lending facility established on December 12, 2007—designed to bypass the primary dealer system while avoiding the discount-window stigma.[4]

Besides not having been able to rely on them as monetary policy conduits, the Fed felt obliged to rescue several primary dealers, and to do so at the expense of solvent banks. When Bear Stearns collapsed in March 2008, the Fed first announced a new Term Securities Lending Facility (TSLF), which would allow primary dealers to borrow securities for up to 28 days from the System Open Market Account so as to be able in turn to employ them as collateral for overnight repo borrowings of Fed funds, made between March 2008 and February 2010 via the Primary Dealer Credit Facility (PDCF). As Robert Eisenbeis (2009: 5) observes, the TSLF served, in effect, to reallocate to primary dealers reserves "that would otherwise have been available to smaller banks or holders of Fed funds to support lending and asset acquisition, with some predictable results for the real economy and economic growth."

Having announced the TSLF, the Fed introduced what was, according to Acharya and Öncü (2010: 337), "its most radical change in monetary policy since the Great Depression," namely, the PDCF. The facility was, essentially, a new discount window for primary dealers. While the old discount window remained relatively quiescent, the new one witnessed an unprecedented volume of lending, most of which took place following Lehman Brothers' September

---

4 According to Armantier et al. (2011), the stigma was such that, after Lehman's failure, banks were willing to pay a premium of at least 150 basis points to acquire funds from the TAF rather than from the discount window.

2008 failure, when the PDCF started to accept risky assets as collateral. According to the Fed's December 2010 disclosure, the heaviest borrowers were banks that were in the greatest peril of failing, including Merrill Lynch, Citigroup, Morgan Stanley, and Goldman Sachs. The accumulated borrowings of each ended up being in the neighborhood of $2 trillion (Sheridan 2011: 13–14), while the total accumulated lending of the PDCF fell just shy of $9 trillion, with a peak of about $150 billion in daily credits during the first week of October 2008.

Finally, starting in November 2008, the Fed began its first round of "quantitative easing," eventually making outright purchases of about $400 million of GSE-guaranteed mortgage-backed securities and (through special purchase vehicles) of another $250 billion in commercial paper and various toxic assets acquired from Bear Sterns and AIG. According to Paul Volcker (2008: 2), these actions took the Fed "to the very edge of its lawful and implied powers, transcending certain long-embedded central banking principles and practices," and testing "the time honored central bank mantra in time of crisis—'lend freely at high rates on good collateral'—to the point of no return." Because the Fed sterilized most of its sub-prime asset purchases, by reducing its Treasury holdings by over

$250 billion and by having the Treasury increase its deposits at the Fed by about $300 billion, the purchases actually reduced the avail- ability of liquid funds to solvent banks. In short, in propping up an operating system that was supposed to help it to act according to Bagehot's advice, the Fed found itself honoring that advice only in the breach.

The Fed's decision to support primary dealers was motivated, not so much by its desire to preserve them as direct agents for monetary policy, but by its fear that their failures could threaten the tri-party repo system by exposing one of the clearing banks to large losses. As Brickler, Copeland, and Martin (2011) explain,

> To give dealers access to their securities during the day, the clearing banks settle all repos early each day, returning cash to cash investors [including the Fed] and collateral to dealers. Because of the delay in settlement, the clearing banks wind up extending hundreds of billions of intraday credit to the dealers until new repos are settled in the evening.

A clearing bank might therefore refuse to continue transacting with a troubled dealer, making it impossible for that dealer to meet its obligations. JPMorgan Chase appears to have taken this step with Lehman, refusing to process its payment instructions and in effect freezing $17 billion in Lehman's assets it held as collateral, the night before Lehman's failure (Duffie 2009: 39). The Fed then worried, not only that other primary dealers were in danger of failing, but that either of the two clearing banks might be exposed to large losses if a large broker-dealer defaulted (Tuckman 2010). The clearing banks themselves thus became "hot spots for systemic risk and taxpayer bailout" (Fricker 2011), and it was largely for their sake that primary dealers were rescued. The rescue of Bear Stearns and the subsequent establishment of the PDCF, in particular, appear to have been motivated not so much by Bear's heavy involvement in the market for mortgage-backed securities as by its status as a big player in the tri-party repo market.

Whether or not they were justified by dealers' systematic importance, the Fed's primary dealer rescues can only have contributed to surviving dealers' inclination—as well as that of the clearing banks—to take excessive risks. As Duffie (2009: 43–44) has observed, "Although the various new government facilities that appeared during the financial crisis of 2007–09 may have prevented some extremely damaging failures, some of these facilities may turn out to be costly to taxpayers and are likely to increase moral hazard in the risk taking of large dealer banks going forward, absent other measures."

The Prescriptions

To improve the Fed's current operating framework and reduce the chances for another financial crisis, I offer the five following prescriptions, all of which embody a Bagehotian perspective: (1) abolish the primary dealer system, (2) limit or abolish repos, (3) abandon "Treasuries only," (4) revive the Term Auction Facility, and (5) stop last-resort discount window lending.

Abolish the Primary Dealer System

The most obvious operating system reform suggested by the crisis is to replace the primary dealer system with one in which numerous financial firms, and perhaps even some nonfinancial firm, take part in the Fed's open market operations.

There are good reasons for the Fed to dispense with its primary dealer system, even putting aside the dangers of relying upon it during crises. "In central banking terms," as Giles and Tett (2008) observe, despite its long pedigree the Fed's primary dealer system "is decidedly old-fashioned," having, as Eisenbeis (2009: 2) explains, "evolved prior to the advent of electronics and computerization of the bid and auction process when institutions relied upon messengers to transmit paper bids to the [System Open Market] Desk." Today, Eisenbeis goes on to observe, there's no reason why a much larger number of qualified firms "could not take part in the daily Open Market transaction process through the System's electronic bidding process." The orthodox arrangement, he adds, "is neither necessary nor in the best interest of taxpayers."

Eisenbeis's conclusion echoes that of a pre-crisis IMF working paper devoted to reviewing the pros and cons of primary dealers for developing countries. According to that paper's authors, Marcone Arnone and George Iden (2003: 8), "automation gives a means to handle large numbers of participants in auctions that was not previously possible," while "electronic markets can offer information on market conditions and prices" that primary dealers were uniquely capable of supplying. Indeed, Arnone and Iden conclude that primary dealers are unnecessary, not just for monetary policy but also for direct sales of government securities, except in less developed economies with as-yet poorly developed securities markets.[5] In short, as a vehicle for the conduct of U.S. monetary policy the primary dealer system is, at best, an anachronism.

The Shadow Financial Regulatory Committee, of which Eisenbeis is a member, has recommended that the Fed take advantage of modern technology to adopt an approach similar to that of the ECB, which routinely conducts open market operations "with more than 500 counterparties throughout the Euro Zone," and which might deal with more than twice as many. Doing so, the committee maintains, "would increase the efficiency of the SOMA transaction process, lower costs, reduce dependence upon a geographically concentrated set of counter parties, and enhance the monetary policy

---

5   A few years earlier McConnachie (1996), observing that there were then no formally designated primary dealers in Australia, Japan, Netherlands, and New Zealand, reached the same conclusion.

transmission process" (Shadow Financial Regulatory Committee 2009). Electronic trading could also preserve the anonymity of firms seeking funds from the Fed.[6] Such improvements, it bears noting, would supply a rationale for doing away with the primary dealer system even if primary dealers' soundness were never in doubt.

So far as outright open market purchases are concerned, there is no reason at all for the Fed to restrict the number of its counterparties, even by limiting participation in open market operations to financial firms, since it doesn't expose itself to counterparty risk in making outright purchases. The only risk it takes on is that connected with depreciation of the securities it acquires, which is of course a function, not of the counterparties it deals with, but of the securities it chooses to buy.

Insofar as they rely upon repos rather than outright security purchases and sales, temporary open market operations pose a somewhat greater challenge, in part because repos, being in effect securitized loans, do expose the Fed to counterparty risk, and so war- rant it in taking measures to guard against such risk. But the view that relying exclusively upon primary dealers is itself such a measure, based as it is on the assumption that primary dealers are "the soundest of sound" financial institutions, is no longer tenable.[7] Instead the opaque nature of broker dealers' undertakings, their high leverage, and the fact that they aren't subject to Fed oversight make such firms particularly risky ones for the Fed to contract with.

Rather than pretend to limit its exposure to the risk of a counterparty's failure by severely limiting the number of counterparties it deals with, the Fed can achieve a genuine reduction in risk by doing just the opposite, diversifying its counterparties so as to greatly reduce its exposure to losses in the event of any single counterparty's failure. A simple way to accomplish this, while further limiting the

---

6 "The central bank should take the lead . . . in encouraging market practices conducive to competitive trading. It could, for instance, encourage a computerized system of bids and offers for securities that protects anonymity" (Axilrod 1997).

7 The failure of MF Global, one of two February 2011 additions to the Fed's primary dealer list, ought to settle any remaining doubts concerning the truth of this declaration. It's worth noting how, even at the time of its admission to the primary dealers club, MF Global was known for being very highly leveraged, and how the Fed waited until October 31st, the date on which MF Global filed for Chapter 11 bankruptcy protection, to terminate its primary dealer status.

Fed's risk exposure and guarding against adverse selection, would be to open participation to any financial institution with a CAMEL score 1 or 2.[8] Such a broadening of Fed counterparties would, as Hoenig (2011: 9) observes, also "enable nearly all banks to play a role in the conduct of monetary policy," leveling the credit allocation playing field while simultaneously making the largest banks considerably less systematically important. Though since the crisis the Fed has agreed to have several new counterparties, including a number of money market funds, take part in reverse repos it eventually intends to employ in mopping up excess base money, it has not otherwise departed from its traditional primary-dealer-based operating framework.[9]

Although counterparty diversification might itself limit clearing banks' exposure to risk in connection with the Fed's repo-op-

---

8   Since the Fed need never advertise its list of banks participating in its open market operations, the procedure need not undermine the confidential nature of CAMEL ratings. On the general reliability of CAMEL ratings as indicators of banks' soundness see Cole and White (2010).

    Counterparty diversification along the lines suggested here seems far prefer- able to the alternative favored by Hoenig (2011: 8), among others, of restoring Glass-Steagall-like provisions to the extent of preventing primary dealers from having commercial bank affiliates. "It is not necessary," Hoenig observes, "that primary dealers be affiliated with banks. It is only necessary that they be institutions that deal in U.S. Treasuries and participate in auctions of U.S. government debt." Hoenig's solution might prevent primary dealers from exploiting genuine economies of scope. Moreover, it was not dealers' involvement in commercial banking, but their other undertakings, that got them in hot water. Neither Lehman Brothers nor Bear Stearns had commercial bank affiliates when they failed.

    A less draconian way, also recommended by Hoenig, to limit risk taking by the Fed's prospective counterparties, and by broker dealers in particular, consists of "rolling back the bankruptcy law for repo collateral to the pre-2005 rules" so as to "discourage the use of mortgage-related assets as [private-market] repo collateral and reduce the potential for repo runs." According to Acharya and Öncü (2010:336), had MBS-based repos been subject to automatic stay, as they would have been under pre-2005 rules, "the Bear Stearns funds could have filed for bankruptcy and the forced fire sale of their assets could have been avoided." As Perottti (2010:4) observes, "bankruptcy exceptions lead to a surrendering of public control over the money supply, which becomes endogenous to the private sector's short-term funding preferences (as any private security may be funded with repo). This high- lights the urgency of measures to contain the private creation of liquidity risk."

9   In its December 14, 2009, report the SFRC criticizes the Fed's move to expand the list of reverse-repo counterparties to include some MMMFs, noting that this move "continues its [the Fed's] dependence upon a small number of institutions and risks creating a two tiered set of money market mutual funds—those that are and those that are not eligible to deal with the desk and potentially eligible for financial support and special treatment during times of financial stress" (Eisenbeis 2009: 2).

erations, the clearing banks would still be heavily exposed to any primary dealer failure, and could consequently remain "hotspots for systemic risk" and for potential Fed operating system failure, through their involvement in the private repo market (Tuckman 2010). Here Chairman Bernanke himself has suggested a solution, consisting of replacing the present private clearing-bank duopoly with a centralized clearing platform or "utility" (Bernanke 2008; see also Singh 2011 and Penney 2011). According to a Financial Economist Roundtable report, the present arrangement

> lacks transparency, has virtually no federal regulatory oversight, raises potential issues of conflicts of interest by virtue of the duopoly's unique access to information on counterparty transactions and ability to meet capital requirements, and poses systemic risks should either of these institutions experience financial distress in their other operations.... If ever there was a question of what firms might be determined too-big-to-fail, the operators of the tri-party repo market fit the bill (Financial Economists Roundtable 2011: 9).

"Policymakers," the report continues, "should explore policies to encourage the movement of tri-party repo transactions to organized exchanges and centralized clearing and settlement systems to eliminate the potential conflicts of interest and systemic risk associated with the present arrangement . . . . The objective should be to avoid the transfer of risk from either of these institutions to the broader market."

Limit or Abolish Repos

A more radical way for the Fed to avoid exposing its operations to repo-related risk would be for it to substantially reduce its use of repos, or even, as Milton Friedman (1982) once proposed, dispense with them altogether.

Repos are convenient devices for conducting temporary open market operations. But they are hardly necessary. Having invented them in 1917, the Fed, as we have seen, largely managed without them until after 1951; and although the Bank of Canada has also been using repos since the 1950s, it was not until the 1990s that other major central banks—including those of England, Japan, Germany Sweden, and Switzerland—began making routine use of them (FRS Study Group 2002: 30). In the United States just prior to the crisis, although repos were the mainstay of the Fed's daily open market operations, they accounted for just 3 percent of the Fed's assets, almost 90 percent of which consisted of outright holdings of U.S. Treasury debt.

The larger the market for the securities in which open market operations are conducted, and the greater the range of maturities available, the more practical it becomes for a central bank to dispense with repos, because a sufficiently deep market allows it to do so without causing unwanted price distortions (Cheun, Köppen-Mertes, and Weller 2009: 11), and because astute management of the SOMA portfolio can provide for a substantial degree of automatic accommodation of seasonal changes in reserve demand without resort to outright sales. The breadth and depth of the market for U.S. Treasuries of all maturities therefore makes the Fed a prime candidate for dispensing with repos.

According to Axilrod (1997: 14), the chief advantage of repos (and reverse repos) compared to outright purchases and sales is that they "tend to enhance liquidity in the underlying securities, helping to develop a more active secondary market" while "encouraging participants to develop as many alternative sources of short-term lending and borrowing as possible." It is hard to resist concluding that, in the United States at least, this advantage is no longer relevant. The market for Treasuries is quite liquid and thick enough, though very large Fed purchases and sales will admittedly still affect their prices and there is surely no need to further encourage private market participants to take advantage of repos for short-term lending and borrowing.

On the contrary: in introducing repos to the U.S. market, the Fed inadvertently encouraged private-market innovations that played a central role in the unfolding of the crisis. "The notion of a repurchase agreement," Henry Liu (2005: 10) trenchantly observed before the crisis,

> was a fiction dreamed up to minimize the impact of such transactions on bank and broker-dealer capital requirements. If these transactions had been called loans, then banks (and broker-dealers) would be required to set aside cash (or perhaps other capital, if a broker-dealer) against such loans.

> By inventing the fiction of calling what is actually a loan by
> some other name, banks and other broker-dealers were able
> to bypass banking regulation and reserve less cash/capital
> against such activities. . . . Repos obviously increase systemic
> risk in the banking system as well as in the monetary system,
> particularly when the daily repos volume has grown to $5 tril-
> lion and is rising by the week.

In developing repos, in short, the Fed played a Frankenstein-like
part, inadvertently transforming primary dealers into so many overleveraged financial industry monsters.

As we have seen, repos do make it easier for the Fed to target interest rates. But this hardly makes them indispensable. On the contrary, it supplies further grounds for reconsidering the Fed's reliance upon a monetary policy instrument that itself appears, in light
of recent experience, to be seriously flawed (see Sumner 2011).

Abandon "Treasuries Only"

Although the proposals so far might be undertaken without al-
tering the Fed's "Treasuries only" policy for open market operations, there are good reasons for combining them with a broadening
of the set of securities used in its temporary, if not in its permanent,
open market operations.[10] In particular, there are good reasons for
having the Fed engage in temporary purchases of some of the private market securities it has traditionally accepted as collateral for
discount window loans, provided that it subjects those securities to
"haircuts" sufficient to protect it against potential credit risk while
otherwise adhering to the classical rule of supplying credit only on
relatively stiff terms.[11]

---

10 Although the Fed has long been legally authorized to purchase securities issued or guar-
anteed by various U.S. government agencies, including the TVA, the Small Business Administration, and the U.S. Postal Service, it made little use of this authority until December 2008, when it began acquiring substantial quantities of housing-agency debt—as
well as much larger quantities of housing-agency mortgage-backed securities.

11 For the relative merits of various private securities for open market operations see Board
of Governors (2002: section 2). Although the Fed offers its desire to avoid credit risk
among reasons for adhering to a Treasury's only rule, the precise threat such risk poses
to it is of a vague sort, since central banks need not be particularly concerned about adverse shocks to their capital, and might even operate temporarily with negative capital
(cf. Bindseil et al. 2004). On the other hand, Steil (2011) points out the limits of a central
bank's ability to function with negative capital without risking hyperinflation.

Conducting open market operations in a variety of securities, and not just in Treasuries, would increase the ability of such operations to take the place of both discount-window lending and emergency credit facilities during financial crises. It would therefore allow the Fed to perform its last-resort lending duties during such crises with- out departing substantially from "business as usual," and especially without allowing the performance of those duties to interfere with the conduct of ordinary monetary policy. An expanded list of securities would also allow the Fed to spread its tri-party repo settlement risk across more than two clearing institutions (Board of Governors 2002, section 2: 3–4). Finally, security diversification would be a natural complement to counterparty diversification: taken together, the two innovations would allow the Fed to satisfy in a straightforward manner Bagehot's requirement that central banks supply liquid funds *freely*, on *any* good collateral—a requirement which (as we have seen) isn't necessarily satisfied by channeling funds through a handful of privileged firms only, and only in exchange for Treasuries.[12]

Here again the ECB supplies a useful counterexample, for it does not normally distinguish between collateral eligible for last- resort (standing facility) lending and collateral eligible for use in its temporary open market operations (Cheun, Köppen-Mertes, and Weller 2009: 18).[13] Partly for this reason, the European system was able to meet the exceptional liquidity needs of the first year of the financial crisis "with relatively few adjustments" to its standard operating framework. The Fed, in contrast, was compelled to intro- duce new collateralized lending programs, including the TAF, TSLF, and PDCF, that served, in effect, to temporarily modify its operating framework so as to make it functionally more akin to the ECB's (Cheun, Köp-

---

12 During the late 1990s and early 2000s the possibility of having the Fed deal in non-Treasury securities was broached in response to the fear that continuing surpluses might render such securities too scarce for the Fed's needs. Although that particular prospect is, unhappily, no longer present, the fact that it might eventually arise again is yet another reason for reconsidering Treasuries only.

13 The ECB ordinarily accepts a variety of euro-denominated private securities, including corporate and bank bonds and mortgage-backed securities, with rating of A- or better, as collateral for both its repos and its standing facility loans. However, in the aftermath of Lehrman's failure it lowered the minimum rating to BBB-.

pen-Mertes, and Weller 2009: 23–25; Duffie 2009: 41).[14]

The Fed's "Treasuries only" policy distinguishes it, not only from most major central banks, but also from its own former self. As David Marshall (2002: 45, 49) observes, at the time of the Fed's establishment its designers equated the purchasing of government debt with "lending to the crown," which they feared would undermine the Fed's independence and open the door to inflation. Consequently, they sought to confine the Fed's credit-granting activities to the dis- counting of commercial paper.[15] Despite this intent, the Fed soon found itself playing handmaiden to the Treasury, until formally released from the obligation to do so by the 1951 Treasury Accord.[16]

One argument against open market operations using private securities is that such purchases are risky. Although outright purchases would not expose the Fed to counterparty risk, even these would expose it to the risk of security issuers' default. It is partly because losses from such defaults ultimately translate into reduced Treasury revenues that Marvin Goodfriend (2010: 6), among others, claims that the Fed should stick to holding risk-free Treasuries. But the argument isn't entirely compelling, because (with respect to repos) the risk can be kept negligible by means of sufficient "haircuts," and because, if last-resort lending is desirable at all—if it is a genuine public good—there's no reason for not having taxpayers shoulder some of the potential cost of providing it, just as they shoulder the cost of supplying emergency assistance to victims of natural disasters. Indeed, the argument for having taxpayers cover losses connected to last-resort lending is the stronger of the two, insofar as such lending may avert a systematic crisis that could end up having financial costs exceeding those of almost any earthquake.

---

14 In contrast, the Fed's later CPFF and TALF programs went "beyond the scope of the Eurosystem's measures," by having the Fed engage in primary-market purchases of commercial paper and by having it take part in what amounted to outright purchases of asset-backed securities (Cheun, Köppen-Mertes, and Weller 2009: 38).

15 The Fed's founders themselves erred, on the other hand, in adhering to the "real bills doctrine"—a doctrine that, besides limiting the sorts of private collateral upon which the Fed was willing to extend credit, caused it to surrender control of monetary policy to a badly programmed "automatic pilot."

16 The scale of the Fed's recent outright Treasury security purchases has, how- ever, revived fears of renewed Fed financing of deficit spending, prompting the Fed and the Treasury to release a March 23, 2009, joint statement reaffirming the Fed's independence.

A second, related argument against Fed purchases of private securities is that such purchases will distort credit markets by favoring certain securities over others. "If the Fed purchases private securities," David Marshall (2002: 52) observes, "it might be seen as selectively approving those obligors whose paper it purchases." It was owing to this concern that the Fed made its final transition to a Treasuries-only policy, between 1977 and 1984, by gradually phasing out purchases of bankers' acceptances.

But a Treasuries-only policy seems neither necessary nor sufficient for the avoidance of Fed favoritism. It isn't necessary because the Fed, rather than arbitrarily favoring certain securities or issuers, might (once again following the ECB's lead—and to some extent that of its own discount-window facility) demarcate a set of eligible securities using various objective criteria, such as issuers' (risk-adjusted) capital and private-agency security ratings; it isn't sufficient because, by dealing with Treasuries only, the Fed plays favorites with the U.S. Treasury.[17]

Here my prescription resembles, and is partly inspired by, Willem Buiter and Anne Sibert's (2007) suggestion that central banks serve as "market makers of last resort," by either buying outright or accepting as repo collateral "systematically important" private financial instruments that have become illiquid, perhaps ceasing to have any market price at all, owing to a breakdown of the markets in which such instruments usually trade. In particular, Buiter (2008a) has proposed that during financial market disruptions the Bank of England (and other central banks, presumably) should offer to purchase or accept as repo collateral "a slightly extended version of what the ECB currently accepts," to wit, any security "rated at least in the single A category." To discover the value of illiquid instruments, and avoid subsidizing their sellers, the Bank can purchase them by means of a "reverse Dutch auction," in which an initial, minimum purchase price is raised progressively until either no buyers are left or the pre-determined purchase amount is met (see also Buiter 2007, 2008b).

---

17 In this respect the "pet securities" argument for Treasuries only reminds one of the similarly question-begging "pet banks" charge leveled at Andrew Jackson when he transferred the government's deposits from the Second Bank of the United States to various state banks.

Buiter and Sibert's proposal has come under criticism for assuming that central banks can, by means of appropriately designed auctions, determine efficient prices even for heterogeneous financial instruments, such as mortgage-backed securities, that lack deep markets and so may not assure multiple auction offers (Smith 2007). My proposal differs both in limiting auctions to such private securities as do not pose the difficulty just mentioned, and in being intended to inform the conduct of open market operations both during crises and in ordinary times, so as to eliminate any need for "emergency" rule changes.

The procedure I have in mind, if only in the crudest of outlines, involves simultaneous reverse (single price) auctions for a set of different securities.[18] The Fed would first have to decide what security types are eligible, favoring those for which holdings are sufficiently dispersed to provide for competitive bidding, and (to further discourage adverse selection) indicating maximum values of total and individual security purchases that it is prepared to make from a single participant.[19] The list of such securities could be compiled, and regularly updated, using reports regularly submitted by prospective counterparties as one requirement for eligibility. Next the Fed would announce the total value of an intended purchase, along with reference prices (reflecting risk-based "valuation haircuts") for particular securities. It would then hold simultaneous reverse auctions, with descending prices *expressed as reference-price percentages*, for each security type, allowing individual counterparties to take part in any or all auctions. The auction continues, through descending-price rounds, until the total nominal value of securities offered at an announced price equals the intended aggregate purchase.

Although this auction procedure may seem cumbersome, thanks to modern technology developing the necessary software to implement it should be well within the Fed's capabilities. Its virtues, as I indicated, are twofold. First, because it pits bidders offering different securities against each other, it can assist in establishing appropriate prices for, and hence enhance the liquidity of, similar

---

18 Some countries, including France, routinely make use of multiple security auctions for primary market issues of government securities.

19 Under the TAF, bidding by individual participants was limited to 10 percent of total amounts being auctioned.

securities that might not themselves qualify for direct Fed purchases. Second and more importantly, it allows the *composition* of open market purchases to adjust automatically with changing market conditions, with few if any central bank purchases of relatively high-risk and long- maturity instruments taking place in normal times, and more such purchases—perhaps substantially more—occurring during times of financial distress. To assure this outcome, and thereby make a single set of open-market rules suffice to consistently conform to Bagehot's rule, while still guarding against adverse selection, the Fed need only take care to set sufficiently low reference prices.[20]

These prescriptions, taken together, might be summarized by paraphrasing Bagehot as follows: the Fed should at all times be prepared to buy good securities freely, outright or subject to repurchase, at competitively determined prices that reflect, but are generally lower than, the values those securities would normally command in the private marketplace.

Revive the Term Auction Facility

A revived TAF, like the one established by the Fed on December 12, 2007, in response to commercial banks' apparent reluctance to borrow from its discount window, and considerably expanded in March 2009, could also serve as a ready-made means for the Fed to implement several of the prescriptions suggested above. Using the TAF the Fed auctioned off predetermined amounts of credit to depository institutions, for terms of either 28 or 84 days, against the same collateral accepted at its discount window, financing the sales by selling Treasury securities. Banks with surplus reserves that were reluctant (owing to perceived counter- party risk) to lend them in the federal funds market, could use the funds to buy the Treasury

---

20 After sketching out my auction plan I discovered much more carefully thought-out proposals in the same spirit by Lawrence Ausubel and Peter Cramton (2008) (for implementing the TARP) and Paul Klemperer (2010) (to assist the Bank of England in combating the post-Northern-Rock credit crunch). In particular, the Ausubel and Cramton proposal goes beyond mine in including enhancements designed to allow for open market purchases of securities for which efficient reference prices are initially unascertainable. In soliciting the Klemperer proposal, the Bank of England asked that the design be one that it could also employ in normal times; in fact it has been using the procedure regularly since the crisis. For further discussion of the challenges involved in designing multiple-security central bank auctions, see Koulischer and Struyven (2011).

securities that the Fed sold, while banks that were short of reserves, but unwilling to borrow from the dis- count window, could bid for TAF funds. So long as the interest the Fed earned on TAF credit exceeded the interest on Treasuries it sold, the program did not expose the Fed to any significant risk, although it did expose taxpayers to potential losses (Goodfriend 2009: 12–13).[21]

Although not, strictly speaking, a vehicle for open market operations, the TAF was something of a cross between such operations and discount window lending: like the former it had counterparties taking part in the auctioning of new reserves, thus allowing borrowers to avoid the stigma connected to discount window borrowing, while let- ting the Fed maintain control of the total stock of bank reserves and limiting its involvement in the allocation of credit. On the other hand the TAF lent on the same relatively generous collateral accepted by the discount window, and was open to depository institutions other than primary dealers.

A shortcoming of the original TAF was that it appeared to violate Bagehot's principles by extending credit at subsidy rather than penalty rates. According to Thornton (2008), whereas the Fed set its discount window primary credit rate at 100 basis points above its tar- get federal funds rate, its lending rate under TAF—the so-called stop-out rate that sufficed to exhaust whatever amount of funds it placed on auction—was often below its primary credit rate. Since the primary credit rate is itself often a subsidy rather than penalty rate, TAF lending was itself effectively subsidized, and TAF for that reason cannot be said to have functioned solely as a vehicle for

---

21 Just how effective TAF was is controversial. Taylor and Williams (2008), Cecchetti (2009), and Mamun, Hassan, and Johnson (2010) claim TAF was ineffective. McAndrews, Sark-ar, and Wang (2008), Christensen, Lopez, and Rudebusch (2009), and Wu (2011) offer more positive appraisals. At least some of the TAF's apparent ineffectiveness appears to stem from the fact that the Fed chose to sterilize TAF lending, financing it, in effect, by selling Treasury securities to prospective lenders in the federal funds market. Consequently, rather than increase the overall supply of liquidity to financial institutions, prior to Lehman's failure the Fed merely forced a reallocation of liquidity to institutions that took advantage of the TAF and PDCF (Thornton 2009a, 2009b). According to Thornton (2009b), if instead the Fed had "pursued a policy of increasing the total supply of credit (the monetary base)," that is, had it engaged in quantitative easing before September 2008, "financial market participants would have been better able to adjust to a decline in house prices," and the failures of Bear Stearns, Lehman Brothers, and AIG as well as the need for TARP might have been avoided.

last- resort lending. To avoid this shortcoming, a revived TAF might maintain a penalty minimum bid rate, while retaining the option of increasing the frequency or size of its auctions when stop-out rates substantially exceed the minimum. Although the presence of such a minimum acceptable bid might prevent the facility from making its announced maximum advance, any difference could be made up by the open market desk, which would in any case have to coordinate its operations with those of the TAF.[22]

Stop Last-Resort Discount Window Lending

It may seem paradoxical to conclude a list of purportedly "Bagehotian" prescriptions by recommending that the Fed altogether cease to engage in direct last-resort lending. But Bagehot wrote at a time when private securities markets were as yet undeveloped, and when central banks made no use at all of open market operations as these are presently understood. Consequently in his day it was only by means of direct lending that the Bank of England could be expected to supply credit "freely" in exchange for good (but mostly unmarketable) collateral.

Today of course all this has changed. Though a "Bagehotian" case can still be made for occasional direct Fed lending so long as the Fed's open market operations are confined, not only to a small number of counterparties but also to a small subset of "good" securities, that case would no longer be valid were the scope of such operations expanded in the manner suggested above. Instead, under such an expanded open market frame- work, direct extended-term lending (as opposed to "adjustment" and seasonal lending) would be more likely than ever to violate Bagehot's Rule, because it would be unlikely to serve any purpose other than to supply credit to individual banks (and perhaps to other firms) that lack good securities of any sort, and are therefore almost certainly insolvent. As Armantier et al. (2011: 27) observe, even under the Fed's present, constrained open- market framework, banks' discount-window visits carry a stigma severe enough to render discount-window lending almost useless as a means for preserving liquidity during financial crises. "One may," they conclude, "question the ability [sic] of the DW [dis-

---

22 For further details concerning how a revived TAF or similar "Auction Credit Facility" might operate, see Board of Governors (2002, section 3: 3–7 and 35–39).

count window] as a channel to supply liquidity simultaneously to a broad set of banks."[23]

Conclusion

In 1873, Bagehot confessed:

> I know it will be said that in this article I have pointed out a deep malady, and only suggested a superficial remedy. I have tediously insisted that the natural system of banking is that of many banks keeping their own cash reserve, with the penalty of failure before them if they neglect it. I have shown that our system is that of a single bank keeping the whole reserve under no effectual penalty of failure. And yet I propose to maintain that system, and only attempt to mend and palliate it.

Today, so might I confess. But while Bagehot saw his remedy as an alternative to radical reform, I see mine as a step toward such reform: by reducing the need for ad-hoc changes to the Fed's operating framework, the prescriptions offered here should make it easier to base monetary policy, including last-resort lending, on strict rules, paving the way in turn toward further, more fundamental reforms that might eventually render the FOMC (and hence the Fed itself, understood as an agency exercising *discretion* over U.S. monetary conditions) obsolete.

---

23 For an intriguing, contrary perspective, see Bindseil and Würtz (2007), who claim that open market operations are dispensable, and that monetary policy might better be implemented by means of standing-facility lending. Besides overlooking the stigma problem connected to standing-facility lending, this argument assumes a lack, not only of last-resort standing-facility credits, but also of overnight ("adjustment") and seasonal credits. The need for the latter types of discount-window lending is, moreover, itself largely a consequence of legal restrictions, including statutory reserve requirements and the Fed's monopoly of paper currency. Concerning the role of reserve requirements see Ely (1997), who observes that the volatility of the federal funds rate is mainly due to "the biweekly scramble of banks . . . to meet their reserve requirements for the just-ended two-week reserve computation period." Concerning currency monopoly as a cause of seasonal credit market pressures in the absence of accommodative central bank policies, see Selgin (1986).

References

Acharya, V. V., and Öncü, T. S. (2010) "The Repurchase Agreement (Repo) Market." In V. Acharya, T. F. Cooley, M. P. Richardson, and I. Walter (eds.) *Regulating Wall Street*, 319–50. Hoboken, N. J.: Wiley (for the New York University Stern School of Business).

Acharya, V., and Skeie, D. (2011) "A Model of Liquidity Hoarding and Term Premia in Inter-Bank Markets." Federal Reserve Bank of New York Staff Report No. 498 (May).

Afonso, G.; Kovner, A.; and Schoar, A. (2011) "Stressed, Not Frozen: The Federal Funds Market in the Financial Crisis." Federal Reserve Bank of New York Staff Report No. 437 (May).

Armantier, O.; Ghysels, E.; Sarkar, A.; and Shrader, J. (2011) "Stigma in Financial Markets: Evidence from Liquidity Auctions and Discount Window Borrowing during the Crisis." Federal Reserve Bank of New York Staff Report No. 483 (January).

Arnone, M., and Iden, G. (2003) "Primary Dealers in Government Securities: Policy Issues and Selected Countries' Experience." IMF Working Paper 03/45 (March).

Ausubel, L. M., and Cramton, P. (2008) "A Troubled Asset Reverse Auction." Working Paper, University of Maryland (5 October).

Axilrod, S. H. (1997) "Transformations to Open Market Operations: Developing Economies and Emerging Markets." International Monetary Fund *Economic Issues* 5 (January).

Bagehot, W. (1873) *Lombard Street: A Description of the Money Market*. London: Henry S. King.

Bernanke, B. S. (2008) "Reducing Systemic Risk." Speech delivered at the Federal Reserve Bank of Kansas City's Annual Economic Symposium, Jackson Hole, Wyo. (22 August).

Bindseil, U.; Camba-Méndez, G.; Hirsch, A.; and Weller, B. (2004) "Excess Reserves and Implementation of Monetary Policy of the ECB." European Central Bank Working Paper Series No. 361 (May).

Bindseil, U., and Würtz, F. (2007) "Open Market Operations: Their Role and Specification Today." In D. G. Myers and J. Toporowski (eds.) *Open Market Operations and Financial Markets*, 54–79. London: Routledge.

Board of Governors of the Federal Reserve System. (1971) "Reappraisal of the Federal Reserve Discount Mechanism." Washington: Board of Governors.

_____ (2002) "Alternative Instruments for Open Market and Discount Window Operations." Washington: Board of Governors.

Brickler, L.; Copeland, A.; and Martin, A. (2011) "Everything You Wanted to Know about the Tri-Party Repo Market, but Didn't Know to Ask." Federal Reserve Bank of New York Liberty Street Blog: http://libertystreeteconomics.newyorkfed org/2011/04.

Buiter, W. H. (2007) "Where the Bank of England Went Wrong, and How to Prevent a Recurrence." Willem Buiter's Maverecon blog.: http://blogs.ft.com/maverecon/2007/11 (17 November).

_____ (2008a) "Wanted: Tough Love from the Central Bank." Willem Buiter's Maverecon blog: http://blogs.ft.com/maverecon/2008/03 (22March).

_____ (2008b) "Central Banks and Financial Crises." Paper presented at the Federal Reserve Bank of Kansas City's symposium on Maintaining Stability in a Changing Financial System, Jackson Hole, Wyo. (21–23 August).

Buiter, W. H., and Sibert, A. (2007) "The Central Bank as a Market Maker of Last Resort." Vox: http://voxeu.org (13 August).

Cecchetti, S. (2009) "Crisis and Responses: The Federal Reserve in the Early Stages of the Financial Crisis." *Journal of Economic Perspectives* 23 (2009): 51–75.

Checchetti, S., and Disyata, T. (2010) "Central Bank Tools and Liquidity Shortages." Federal Reserve Bank of New York *Economic Policy Review* (February): 1–17.

Cheun, S.; Köppen-Mertes, I. von; and Weller, B. (2009) "The Collateral Frameworks of the Eurosystem, the Federal Reserve System and the Bank of England and the Financial Market Turmoil." European Central Bank *Occasional Paper* 107 (December).

Christensen, J. H.; Lopze, J. A.; and Rudebusch, G. D. (2009) "Do Central Bank Liquidity Facilities Affect Interbank Lending Rates?" Federal Reserve Bank of San Francisco Working Paper 2009–13.

Cole, R. A., and White, L. J. (2010) "Déjà Vu All Over Again: The Causes of U.S. Commercial Bank Failures *This* Time Around." *Journal of Financial Services Research* (forthcoming).

Duffie, D. (2009) "The Failure Mechanics of Dealer Banks." Working Paper, Stanford University (22 June).

_____ (2010) *How Big Banks Fail, and What to Do about It.* Princeton, N.J.: Princeton University Press.

Dunne, P. G.; Fleming, M.; and Zholos, A. (2009) "Repo Market Microstructure in Unusual Monetary Policy Conditions." Working Paper (16 December).

Eisenbeis, R. A. (2009) "The Financial Crisis: Miss-Diagnosis and Reactionary Responses." Working Paper.

Ely, B. (1997) "Time to Abolish Reserve Requirements." *The Golembe Report* No. 7 (27 August): www.cais.com/ely/ tgr82797.htm.

Federal Reserve System Study Group (2002) "Alternative Instruments for Open Market and Discount Window Operations." Washington: Board of Governors of the Federal Reserve System (December).

Financial Economists Roundtable (2011) "How to Manage and Help to Avoid Systemic Liquidity Risk."

Fisher, R. W., and Rosenblum, H. (2009) "The Blob That Ate Monetary Policy." *Wall Street Journal* (27 September).

Fricker, M. (2011) "Let's Get Going on the Real Story of the Financial Crisis: Securitized Banking." SABEW: http://sabew.org/2011/05.

Friedman, M. (1960) *A Program for Monetary Stability.*
New York: Fordham University Press.

_____ (1982) "Monetary Policy: Theory and Practice." *Journal of Money, Credit, and Banking* 14: 98–118.

Giles, C., and Tett, G. (2008) "Lessons of the Credit Crunch."
Financial Times (FT.com, 11 February).

Goodfriend, M. (2009) "Central Banking in the Credit Turmoil: An Assessment of Federal Reserve Practice." Working Paper, Carnegie-Mellon University.

Goodfriend, M., and King, R. G. (1988) "Financial Deregulation, Monetary Policy, and Central Banking." Federal Reserve Bank of Richmond *Economic Review* (May/June): 3–22.

Goodfriend, M., and Lacker, J. M. (1999) "Limited Commitment and Central Bank Lending." Federal Reserve Bank of Richmond *Economic Quarterly* 85 (Fall): 1–27.

Hetzel, R. L. (2009) "Government Intervention in Financial Markets: Stabilizing or Destabilizing?" Working Paper, Federal Reserve Bank of Richmond.

Hoenig, T. M. (2011) "Do SIFIs Have a Future?" Paper presented at the NYU-Stern School of Business Conference, "Dodd-Frank One Year On," Washington (27 June).

Humphrey, T. M. (1986) "The Real Bills Doctrine." In T. M.

Humphrey, *Essays on Inflation.* 5th ed., 80–90. Richmond: Federal Reserve Bank of Richmond.

Kaufman, G. G. (1991) "Lender of Last Resort: A Contemporary Perspective."
Journal of Financial Services Research 5 (2): 95–110.

_____ (1999) "Do Lender of Last Resort Operations Require Bank Regulation?" Presented at a Conference on "Is Bank Regulation Necessary?" American Enterprise Institute, Washington (27 October).

Klemperer, P. (2010) "The Product-Mixed Auction: a New Auction Design for Differentiated Goods." *Journal of the European Economic Association* 8 (May): 526–36.

Kohn, D. L. (2009) "Policy Challenges for the Federal Reserve." Speech delivered at the Kellogg School of Management, Northwestern University (16 November).

Koulischer, F., and Struyven, D. (2011) "Central Bank Liquidity Auctions and Collateral Quality." Working Paper (October). Lacker, J. M. (2004) "Payment System Disruptions and the Federal Reserve Following September 11, 2001." *Journal of Monetary Economics* 51: 935–65.

Liu, H. C. K. (2005) "The Wizard of Bubbleland, Part 3: How the U.S. Money Market Really Works." *Asia Times* (27 October).

Marshall, D. (2002) "Origins of the Use of Treasury Debt in Open Market Operations: Lessons for the Present." Federal Reserve Bank of Chicago *Economic Perspectives* 26 (First Quarter): 45–54.

McAndrews, J.; Armantier, O.; and Krieger, S. (2008) "The Federal Reserve's Term Auction Facility." Federal Reserve Bank of New York *Current Issues in Economics and Finance* 14 (5): 1–10.

McAndrews, J.; Sarkar, A.; and Wang, Z. (2008) "The Effect of the Term Auction Facility on the London Inter-Bank Offered Rate." Working Paper, Federal Reserve Bank of New York (1 May).

McConnachie, R. (1996) *Primary Dealers in Government Securities Markets. Handbook in Central Banking,* No. 6. London: Bank of England Centre for Central Banking Studies.

Mamum, A.; Hassan, M. K.; and Johnson, M. (2010) "How Did the Fed Do? An Empirical Assessment of the Fed's New Initiatives in the Financial Crisis." *Applied Financial Economics* 20 (1–2): 15–30.

Penney, J. (2011) "Out of the Shadows: Central Clearing of Repo, a Transparent Market Structure for Cash Borrowers and Lenders." McKinsey & Company (August).

Perotti, E. (2010) "Systemic Liquidity Risk and Bankruptcy." Centre for Economic Policy Research, Policy Insight No. 52 (October).

Schwartz, A. J. (1992) "The Misuse of the Fed's Discount Window." Federal Reserve Bank of St. Louis *Review* (September/October): 58–69.

Selgin, G. (1986) "Accommodating Changes in the Relative Demand for Currency: Free Banking versus Central Banking." *Cato Journal* 6 (2): 617–34.

Selgin, G.; Lastrapes, W. D.; and White, L. H. (2010) "Has the Fed Been a Failure?" Cato Institute Working Paper No. 2. Forthcoming in *Journal of Macroeconomics.*

Shadow Financial Regulatory Committee (2009) "Reforming the Primary Dealer Structure." Statement No. 280 (14 December). Sheridan, B. (2011) "Lender of Last Resort: An Examination of the Federal Reserve's Primary Dealer Credit Facility." Working Paper, University of Note Dame.

Singh, M. (2011) "Making OTC Derivatives Safe: A Fresh Look." IMF Working Paper No. 11–66. Washington: International Monetary Fund.

Smith, Y. (2007) "Gotcha! (Willem Buiter's Market Maker of Last Resort Edition)." Available at www.nakedcapitalism.com/2007/12/ gotcha-willem-buiters-market-maker-of.html (15 December).

Steil, B. (2011) "No, Brad DeLong, There Is No Draghi Claus." *Forbes Online* (8 December).

Sumner, S. (2011) "Can the Fed Learn to Speak a Non–Interest Rate Language?" *The Money Illusion* (30 October): www.themoney illusion.com/?p=11586.

Taylor, J. B., and Williams, J. C. (2008) "A Black Swan in the Money Market." Federal Reserve Bank of San Francisco Working Paper No. 2007–46.

Thornton, D. L. (2008) "Walter Bagehot, the Discount Window, and TAF." Federal Reserve Bank of St. Louis *Economic Synopsis* No. 17.

_____ (2009a) "The Fed, Liquidity, and Credit Allocation." Federal Reserve Bank of St. Louis *Review* (January/February): 13–21.

_____ (2009b) "Would Quantitative Easing Sooner Have Tempered the Financial Crisis and Economic Recession?" Federal Reserve Bank of St. Louis *Economic Synopsis* No. 37.

Tuckman, B. (2010) "Systemic Risk and the Tri-Party Repo Clearing Banks." Center for Financial Stability Policy Paper (February). Volcker, P. (2008) Speech before the Economic Club of New York (8 April).

Wu, T. (2011) "The U.S. Money Market and the Term Auction Facility in the Financial Crisis of 2007–2009." *Review of Economics and Statistics* 93 (2): 617–31.

Reflections on The Case for the True Gold Standard

Lew Lehrman

Fundamentals[1]

Gold is a fundamental, metallic element of the earth's chemical constitution. Its essential chemical composition reveals perfect integrity, homogeneity, and fungibility. Gold exhibits unique properties which enabled it, during two millennia of market testing, to emerge as a universally accepted store of value, medium of exchange, and throughout history to sustain stable purchasing power over the long run. Rarely considered in monetary debates, the natural properties of gold caused it to prevail as a stable monetary standard by means of which trading peoples worldwide could make trustworthy direct and indirect exchanges for all other articles of wealth. The preference of tribal cultures, as well as ancient and modern civilizations, to use gold as money was no mere accident of history. Nor has this natural, historic, and global preference for gold—as a store of value and standard of measure—been easily purged by academic theories and government fiat.

Consider the natural properties of gold. Gold is durable, homogenous, and fungible. Indeed, by its intrinsic scientific nature, gold is imperishable, indestructible, and malleable. Gold has a relatively low melting point, facilitating coinage. Gold is portable and can be readily transported from place to place in exchange for other articles of wealth. Large and small quantities of gold can be safely stored at low cost and then exchanged for redeemable, convertible, and convenient monetary certificates, bank deposits, and notes. Convertible bills of exchange, bank notes, and bank deposits efficiently extended the gold standard worldwide.

Like paper, gold is almost infinitely divisible into smaller denominations. But unlike the near-zero marginal cost of producing paper money, gold—like other articles of wealth in the market—requires

---

1 For this essay the evidence, sources, differing interpretations, and specific author references (and bibliography) will be found in the second and revised edition of Lewis E. Lehrman *The True Gold Standard - A Monetary Reform Plan without Official Reserve Currencies*, published August 2012.

real labor and capital to be produced. The real labor and capital invested in producing a unit of gold is an objective value proportional to the objective labor and capital invested in producing a unit of all other products and services in the market for which real money, gold, might be exchanged. Prices for products and services vary with subjective preferences. But the real costs of production persist as an objective, underlying market regulator of the subjective prices of goods and services. Despite subjective preferences, a mutual exchange between the gold monetary unit and other goods and services is a transparent, proportional, equitable exchange – grounded by real costs of production – among producers and consumers, between owners of capital and owners of labor.

But almost no marginal labor and capital is required to produce an additional unit of paper money. Thus, legal tender paper money is subject only to quantitative control, and the discretion of political authorities. Historical evidence shows that inconvertible paper money is overproduced—tending always toward depreciation and inflation—interrupted by bouts of austerity and inflation. Over the long run, the historical evidence also shows that the exchange of forced and spurious paper money for the products of real labor and capital has not maintained equitable exchanges between labor and capital in the market. Market exchanges based on depreciating paper money and floating paper currencies always lead to speculative privilege of insiders, generally the financial class, thus to injustice in exchange – whereas the gold monetary standard, requiring real labor and capital to be produced, sustains equitable exchange by maintaining its long-run purchasing power against a standard assortment of goods.

Because of its imperishability and density of value per weight unit, gold can be held and stored (saved) permanently – at incidental carrying costs per unit of value. Precious metal monetary tokens (gold and silver) survived millennia of monetary experiments with inferior or perishable alternatives such as shells, grains, cattle, tobacco, base metals, and many other monetary tokens which are either consumed, perishable, bulky or of insufficient value for large-scale commercial exchange over long distances. For example, perishables are not storable for long periods at very low cost; nor are they portable cheaply over long distances to exchange for other goods; nor are they useful and efficient to settle short-and long-term debts promptly.

The high value but relatively low melting point of gold, compared to other precious metals, caused it to emerge in the market as the most marketable, practical monetary coin of enduring, efficient, commercial utility. A single ounce of gold is one of the most densely packed elemental values drawn from the Earth's crust. Its relative scarcity, imperishability, marketability, and aesthetic desirability sustained it in the market as preferred money, not least because, unlike paper money, the cost of real factors of production were required to produce it for the purpose of market exchange – or saving, or adornment (a form of durable saving). Through a process of long-term economic evolution in tribal, interregional, and national trading markets, gold's natural properties became known in almost all cultures, accounting for the fact that gold became universally marketable and acceptable as the optimum, long-term store of value and uniform standard of commercial measure and medium of exchange. Universal marketability and acceptability is a hallmark of global money. Silver, with its much lower value per unit of weight, was the sub-optimal monetary metal of modern civilization, exhibiting as it does many but not all of the properties required of large-scale international exchange and payments.

Merchants, bankers, farmers, and laborers may not have self-consciously considered these facts, but over the long run they behaved as if they did. Desired by everyone, trading peoples learned that gold was the most marketable article of wealth in the market. Thus, for the purpose of indirect exchange, gold was especially desired as the least imperfect medium of exchange. People, even hostile nations, freely accepted gold from one another in exchange for other goods. Unlike depreciating, inconvertible paper money manipulated by politicians, gold was an unimpeachable, non-national, universally accepted money which could be held as reserves, and passed on as a reliable store of stable future purchasing power. All who cherished the value and purchasing power of their saved labor – pensioners, working people, those on fixed incomes – came to rely on the gold monetary standard as a stable, long-term proxy for a standard assortment of goods and services to be purchased later, perhaps much later.

Today's global stock of aboveground gold in all its forms approximates five- to six-billion ounces – perhaps more – close to one ounce per capita of the world population. This is similar to the ratio of the gold stock to population in past centuries. Because of gold's lasting value from time immemorial, and the human incentive to conserve all scarce resources, these five- to six-billion ounces of aboveground gold represent most of the gold ever produced. So densely packed is the value of gold that the aboveground gold stock today may be enclosed in a cube of approximately seventy (70) feet on each side. This fact, combined with gold's low melting point makes it clear that gold money, en masse, may be easily converted to substantial amounts of circulating monetary coin, the reliable means by which to guarantee convertible paper for exchange in the market.

Moreover, the empirical data of monetary history demonstrate that the stock of aboveground gold has grown for centuries in direct proportion to the growth of population and output per capita. As with all desired goods and services offered at free prices in the market it requires enterprise, intelligence, and work to produce sufficient growth of the desired gold stock by which to accommodate economic growth and to maintain a stable, long-term price level. To that end, the average, annual, long-run growth of the stock of gold in the modern world approximates 1.5% of the total aboveground stock of gold. This remarkable fact accounts for the unique, long-run stability of the purchasing power of gold. New output of gold money, joined to its rate of turnover (MV), is sufficient for both economic growth and long-run stability of the general price level, as there is not so much new output of gold by which to affect, over the long run, the relative value of the existing stock of gold. In a word, the ordered, modest, long-run growth of the gold stock paralleled the gradual growth of population and economic output per capita. This hidden-but-crucial commercial equation of the social order was a fundamental reason why the true gold standard, i.e., gold-based money, became the foundation of the stable monetary institutions of modern market civilization. Gold-based money not only stabilized the long-term price level, but its network effects integrated and compounded the growth of the advanced, competitive trading nations of the Western world during the vast, free market, Industrial Revolution of the 19th century. For the purpose of global trade and exchange currencies convertible to the gold monetary standard had engirdled the earth by the beginning of the 20th century.

As the technology and productivity of the payments mechanism evolved—bringing banknotes and checking account deposits (among other credit and monetary transfer mechanisms) into modern monetary circulation—these substitute monetary tokens, convertible to gold, gradually economized the use and transfer, for settlement purposes, of the gold monetary standard in the growing world economy. But these banknotes and checks, all credit instruments, derived and sustained their value and acceptability because, at the time of their origin and subsequently, all knew they were credit instruments convertible to gold. Still, gold transfers were mostly used to settle residual balance-of-payments deficits, a necessary and efficient adjustment mechanism by which to rebalance domestic and international trade and exchange.

Despite legal tender paper money, and the disabilities presently imposed on gold by the political authorities, gold retains the same inherent properties which still make it the least imperfect monetary standard of the market. Indeed, all inconvertible paper money systems, based on contemporary fractional reserve banking, use the vestigial forms but not the substance of their original convertible currency systems.

In sum, gold is natural money – not least because it combines in a single, indestructible substance the primary functions of money – a standard unit of account, a stable medium of exchange, a stable store of value, a stable deferred means of payment. By combining the essential functions of money into one stable, real, and imperishable monetary token, the market guided the authorities over time to bestow on gold coin the status of an official monetary standard. This consolidation of monetary functions attained unique economies of scale for the gold standard. As a globally accepted standard, gold money was moreover endowed thereby with the profound-but-simple national and international networking effects by which digital free prices could be communicated worldwide. Thus, the gold standard exhibited economies of global information scale, a recognizable virtue in the present electronic age of global digital standards. The adoption of the gold standard by the major trading nations in the nineteenth century led to a radical reduction in the settlement costs of international trade and transactions—a crucial confidence and reliability factor stimulating an unparalleled boom in international trade, constantly rebalanced globally by residual deficit settlements in gold.

A Just Social Order and Economic Growth

To choose or to reject the true gold standard is to choose on the one hand a free, just, stable, and objective monetary order; or on the other, to embrace manipulated, floating paper money, the fundamental cause of a casino culture of speculation and crony capitalism—with the incipient financial anarchy and inequality it engenders. Only currencies convertible to gold can be indispensable safe guards of the value of wages and savings of all working people.

Restoration of a dollar convertible to gold rebuilds a necessary financial incentive for real, long-term, economic growth by means of increased saving, increasing investment per capita, and entrepreneurial innovation and capital allocation in productive facilities. Thus does convertibility lead to rising employment and rising real wages underwritten by a stable, long-term price level – reinforced domestically, as it should be, by a more stable banking system – subject to the rule of convertibility – and internationally, by stable exchange rates mutually convertible to gold. Consider the past decade of hyper-managed paper currencies and manipulated floating exchange rates wherein American economic growth has fallen to 1.7%, at an average annual rate. Under the classical gold standard, U.S. economic growth averaged 3-4% annually over the long run, the equal of any period in American history.

Differential growth rates are not mere accidents of history. The gold dollar, or true gold standard, underwrites, among other things, just and lasting purchasing power for workers, savers, investors, and entrepreneurs. It prevents recurring, massive distortions in relative prices by manipulated paper currencies and floating exchange rates which misallocate scarce resources. It minimizes the enormous speculative capital flows characteristic of floating-paper currency systems. It rules out the "exorbitant privilege" and insupportable burden of official reserve currencies.

The gold standard and bankruptcy are two rule-based market institutions which limit and regulate the abuse of fractional reserve banking under inconvertible paper-money systems. It reduces to a minimum the enormous premium exacted by the banker and broker establishment in the purchase and sale of volatile foreign exchange. Convertibility thus tends toward stable long-run domestic and international growth – not austerity. It rewards long-term savings, entrepreneurial innovation, growing investment per capita, and rising worker productivity. It suppresses the incentives for pure financial speculation under manipulated paper currencies and floating exchange rates. Moreover, the lawfully defined gold content of a stable currency encourages long-term lending and investment – more reliance on equity, less on debt. With currencies convertible to gold, long-term lenders receive in turn, say after thirty years, similar purchasing power—measured by a standard assortment of goods and services—compared to the capital or credit they surrendered to the borrowers thirty years ago to make long-term investments. This fact is confirmed by the empirical data of the classical gold standard (1879-1914).

A dollar convertible to gold by law, reinforced by effective bankruptcy law, sustains economic justice—regulating and disciplining speculative capital, restraining political and banking authorities such that they cannot lawfully depreciate the present value or the long-term purchasing power of lagging dollar wages, savings, pensions, and fixed incomes. Nor under the sustained, legal restraint of convertibility can governments ignite major, long-run, credit and paper money inflations with their subsequent debt deflations. Under the gold standard, the penalty of excessive corporate and banking leverage is insolvency and bankruptcy. As the profits belong to the owners, so should the losses. Bankruptcy of insolvent firms shields the taxpayer from the burden of government bailouts. Under the rule-based gold standard in a free market order managers, stockholders, and bondholders must bear the responsibility for insolvency. In the absence of currency convertibility and bankruptcy, crony capitalism corrupts and commandeers free markets.

A major virtue of restoration of currency convertibility to gold is neglected by contemporary economists. A stable dollar leads to increased saving not only from income, but also from dishoarding – releasing a vast reservoir of savings previously hoarded in the form of inflation hedges such as commodities, art, farmland and other vehicles – all purchased to protect against the ravages of inflation. These trillions of hoarded savings, imprisoned in hedging vehicles by uncertainty and inflation, are induced out of speculative hedges by currency convertibility to gold. The savings are then supplied in the market to entrepreneurs, business managers, and households to create new income-generating investment in production facilities, thereby leading to increased employment and productivity. On the other hand, sustained central bank subsides to government, and government-subsidized consumption, both enabled by inconvertible paper and credit money, lead – through deficit financing, transfer payments, paper money fiscal and monetary stimulation – to disinvestment, debt financing, speculative privilege, and growing inequality of wealth.

It is rarely considered by conventional academic opinion that the long-term stability of a rule-based currency convertible to gold brings about a major mutation in human behavior. In a free market every able-bodied person and firm must first make a supply to the market before making a demand. This social and economic principle effectively alters human conduct. It encourages production before consumption, balances supply and demand, rules out inflation, maintains balanced international trade, and upholds the framework for economic growth and stable money. In a free market, grounded by the rule of convertibility to gold, new money and credit may be prudently issued only against new production or additional supply for the market, thus maintaining equilibrium between total demand and total supply – a necessary condition of stable money and a stable general price level. Moreover, worldwide hoarding, caused by government and bank over-issue of inconvertible paper and credit money, comes to an end. Antiques, art, commodities, diamonds, jewelry, and innumerable other vehicles mobilized as hedges to cope with depreciating currencies will be disgorged for real money, then mobilized for investment, as the reality of an authentic and trustworthy monetary standard takes hold in a free market worthy of the name.

By means of currencies mutually convertible to gold, people and firms worldwide will have regained the confidence to embrace the convenience of convertible currencies with which to invest profitably in productive facilities and the jobs to work them. *The irony of the gold standard and currency convertibility is that it ends speculation in gold.* It restores the incentive to use and to hold convertible paper currency and other credit-based forms of cash balances. Currency convertibility to gold limits not only the extent of inflation, but, by the same mechanisms the gold standard also limits its twin sibling, deflation.

Rebalancing the Global Economy

The overall balance-of-payments of a country, or a currency area, is in deficit when more money is paid abroad than received; a surplus occurs when more money is received by a country or currency area than paid abroad. The United States, because of the dollar's role as the reserve currency of the world, has experienced an overall balance-of-payments deficit most of the past half-century and, over that full period, systemic inflation. When there are substantial unemployed resources in the U.S. economy, inflation of the general price level occurs gradually; but at full employment, rapidly.

Under both the Bretton Woods agreement (1944-71) and the subsequent floating, dollar-based, global reserve currency system the U.S. budget and balance-of-payments deficits have been financed substantially by U.S. government trust funds, the Federal Reserve, and by foreign purchases of dollars flooding abroad. Since 2008 the budget and balance-of-payments deficits were accompanied by unprecedented quantitative easing, a euphemism for large-scale central bank money and credit creation (or "money printing"). By this means the Fed finances not only the budget and balance-of-payments deficits, but also overleveraged banks, insolvent debtors, and other wards of the state. But we observe that when the Fed slows quantitative easing (money printing), deflation threatens.

Under the dollar-based reserve currency system, the U.S. balance-of-payments deficit causes Fed-created dollars to rush abroad – directed there by relative price differences. In foreign countries, much of these excess dollars are monetized by foreign monetary authorities and held as official, foreign exchange reserves. But these official dollar reserves of foreign countries are not inert. They do not lie around in bank vaults. They are in fact reinvested in the U.S. dollar market – especially in U.S. government securities sold to finance the federal budget deficit. In effect, the United States exports its debt securities, in exchange for the dollars it created and used to settle its balance-of-payments deficits abroad. Everything goes on as if there were no U.S. budget or balance-of-payments deficits. No adjustment is required of the United States to settle its debts, or to rebalance deficits with surpluses. Thus, the world dollar standard enables America to buy without really paying.

Rebalancing world trade is impossible under an official reserve currency system. (The IMF and the central banks are pathetic shadows of "all the king's men" trying to put Humpty Dumpty, that is global rebalancing, back together again.) This perverse monetary system, whereby the reserve currency country issues its own money to finance and refinance its increasing deficits and debts, augments global purchasing power and potential inflation, because the newly issued money is not associated with newly produced goods and services. Total demand has been divorced from supply. When total demand exceeds total supply, engineered by quantitative easing, inflation generally occurs first in marketable and scarce commodities, equities, and inflation hedges – other general price level effects to be deferred in the CPI because of unemployed labor and other unutilized resources. Ultimately, the general price level will rise as the economy approaches full employment. (A special factor in 2011-2012, mitigating the general price level effect of money printing, has been the worldwide panic demand for the dollar, and the desire to hold the dollar in cash equivalents, rather than to spend or invest it.)

Under the rule-based gold standard, settlement transfers of gold money effectively require adjustment of balance-of-payments deficits, re-establishing equilibrium among trading nations. The regular settlement of payments deficits eliminates a root cause of global imbalances. Under the true gold standard, residual balance-of-payments deficits could no longer be settled in newly issued national paper and credit monies, such as the reserve currencies of the dollar or euro. Instead, residual balance-of-payments deficits among nations would be settled with an impartial, non-national monetary standard – gold. The requirement to settle in gold promptly rules out the exponential debt increases of flawed reserve currency systems, one example of which was the gold-exchange standard of the 1920s, the collapse of which turned a recession into the Great Depression. Under the true gold standard, without official reserve currencies, rebalancing of the world trading system is a function of an efficient, international, adjustment mechanism engendered by prompt settlement of deficits.

Moreover, it is very much in the American national interest to terminate the reserve currency role of the dollar, for it is an insupportable burden borne by the United States since the end of World War II (even since the Great Power Genoa agreement of 1922). The U.S. taxpayer should no longer go further into debt in order to supply the world with dollar reserves denominated in U.S. debt. Terminating the "privilege" and the burden of the official reserve currency role of the dollar, combined with the restoration of dollar convertibility to gold, brings gradually to an end the long era of extreme global trade imbalances, secular debt accumulation and inflation, and currency depreciation. Furthermore, because the reserves of monetary authorities are to be held only in gold and domestic currency claims, the exchange-rate risk is eliminated in all national banking systems formerly dependent on official, foreign currency reserves.

The rule-based, true gold standard not only ends the official reserve currency role of the dollar, but it also limits arbitrary Federal Reserve money issuance secured by spurious and illiquid collateral. Unstable mutations in the true (or classical) gold standard of the past – including the failed "gold-exchange" system of Bretton Woods and the collapse of its predecessor, the "gold-exchange standard" of the 1920s and 1930s – must be ruled out. So, too, must floating exchange rates. For almost a century, policy makers, politicians, historians, and economists have confused the flawed interwar gold-exchange standard, based on official reserve currencies, with the true or classical gold standard. Establishment economists and historians have mistakenly blamed the Great Depression on the gold standard, instead of on the liquidation of the gold-exchange system and the official reserve currency system, first established at Genoa in 1922 – which then, like Banquo's ghost, reappeared in 1944 in the in the form of the Bretton Woods system.

The Bretton Woods pegged exchange rate system, based on the official reserve currency role of the dollar, collapsed in 1971 because the United States had accumulated more short-term debt to foreigners than it was willing to redeem in gold. The collapse of the Bretton Woods system in 1971, based on the official reserve currency role of the dollar, ushered in the worst American economic decade since the 1930s. The unemployment rate at the end of a decade in 1982 was higher even than the unemployment rate occasioned by the collapse of the Fed-induced real estate bubble of 2007-09. Similarly, the recession of 1929-30 became the Great Depression of the 1930s because of the collapse and liquidation of the interwar official reserve currency system – based as it was on the pound and the dollar. The liquidation of official sterling and dollar currency reserves deflated the world banking system because without those reserves the banks were forced to deleverage, call in loans, or go bankrupt. Banks worldwide did all three.

Since 1971, the floating exchange rate system, or the world dollar standard, has been even more perverse and crisis-prone than the reserve currency systems of Bretton Woods and of the interwar era. Indeed, the privilege and the burden of the dollar's role as the world's official reserve currency has been a cause not only of extreme inflation and the subsequent threat of deflation, but also of industrial and manufacturing displacement in the United States. The world dollar standard is a primary cause of declining U.S. competitiveness, one witness of which is the collapse of the international net investment position of the United States. In 1980, the U.S. net international investment position was 10% of GDP. In 2010 it was negative 20% of GDP. The difference was equal to the increase of foreign-held official dollar reserves, arising from continuous U.S. balance-of-payments deficits under the dollar-based official reserve currency system.

Under the present official reserve currency system the perennial U.S. balance-of-payments deficit will, more often than not, continue to flood foreign financial systems and central banks with undesired dollars – followed by brief periods of dollar scarcity, the threat of deflation, and a cyclical rise of the dollar on foreign exchanges. Foreign monetary authorities may continue to purchase excess dollars against the issue of new domestic money, thus duplicating potential purchasing power un-associated with the production of new goods – tending to sustain worldwide inflation, followed by recession and the threat of deflation. So-called sterilization techniques designed to neutralize foreign exchange inflows are not fully effective. Without monetary reform, the excess dollars purchased by foreign central banks – reinvested in U.S. government securities and other dollar debt – will continue to finance excess consumption and rising government spending in the United States.

In 2012, inflation of the general price level (or CPI) proceeds gradually in the United States because of unemployed resources. At full employment, inflation will pick up. But then, if the Fed and the banking system abruptly reduce the growth rate of credit, the threat of deflation will reappear (as in 2006-07). Because the reserve currency system generally leads to a rapid increase in global purchasing power, without a commensurate increase in the supply of goods and services, the systemic tendency of the reserve currency system is monetary expansion or inflation – at first in the prices of investment assets, commodities, and speculative vehicles like art and antiques. Yet the process can dangerously work in reverse, causing deflation, especially when the Fed tightens, or there is panic out of foreign currencies into the dollar (the Asian Crisis, 1996-2002, and the Euro Crisis – 2012). Illiquidity abroad causes foreign official dollar reserves to be resold or liquidated in very large quantities, reducing the global monetary base – as occurred in 1929-33 and recently in 2007-09.

In the absence of government prohibitions and restrictions in favor of inconvertible paper and credit money, the historical evidence shows that gold—or paper and credit money convertible to gold—was preferred and accepted in trade and exchange from time immemorial. Until recent times the classical gold standard also underwrote, indeed required, global trade rebalancing—now the subject of empty exhortations by the IMF and political authorities. But to desire a goal without the effective means to attain it—namely, the true gold standard–is to court political and financial disaster. In the absence of prompt balance-of-payments settlements in gold, the undisciplined official reserve currency systems have immobilized the international adjustment mechanism with the result being increasing trade imbalances, ever-rising debt and credit leverage at home and abroad. Under the world dollar standard, other nations have gained desired dollar reserves only as the United States becomes an increasingly leveraged debtor through balance-of-payments deficits; whereas under the gold standard, the global economy may actually attain balance-of-payments surplus as a whole vis-à-vis worldwide gold producers. Among its monetary virtues—as the least imperfect monetary system of civilization—the true gold standard, without official reserve currencies is the sole, rule-based monetary order which reliably and systematically rebalances worldwide trade and exchange among all participating nations.

How to Get From Here to There

Step 1. *America leads by the President announcing unilateral resumption of the gold monetary standard at a date certain, not more than four years in the future.* Unilateral resumption means that the U.S. dollar will be defined by law as a certain weight unit of gold. The Treasury, the Federal Reserve, and the entire banking system will be obligated to maintain the gold value of the dollar. On the date of congressionally authorized resumption – that is, unrestricted dollar-gold convertibility – Federal Reserve banknotes and U.S. dollar bank demand deposits will be redeemable in gold on demand at the statutory gold parity. Further use by foreign governments of the dollar as an official reserve currency will entail no legal recognition by the United States. U.S. law will be equipped to deal with countries which attempt systematically to undervalue their currencies.

Step 2. The President issues an executive order eliminating every and all taxes imposed on the buying, selling, and circulation of gold. The President issues an executive order providing for the issuance of Treasury bonds backed by a proportional weight of gold. Since Federal Reserve notes and bank deposits (money) are not taxed by any jurisdiction, the executive order specifies that gold, being legal tender money may not be taxed in any jurisdiction of the United States, nor abroad. Gold can be used to settle all debts, public and private. The Treasury and authorized private mints will provide for the minting and wide circulation of legal tender gold coin in appropriate denominations, free of any and all taxation.

Step 3. Shortly after the Announcement (Step 1), the United States calls for an International Monetary Conference of interested nations to provide for the deliberate wind up of the dollar-based, official reserve currency system – and the consolidation and refunding of foreign official dollar reserves. The international agreement to be negotiated will inaugurate the reformed international monetary system, that is, multilateral currency convertibility of major countries to the gold monetary standard, without official reserve currencies. Stable exchange rates would be the result. The value of each participating currency would be a function of its stipulated gold parity.

Step 4. The conference – attended by representatives of the BIS, IMF, WTO, and the World Bank – would establish gold as the means by which nations would settle residual balance-of-payments deficits. The international agreement would designate gold, in place of reserve currencies, as the internationally recognized monetary reserve asset. Official foreign currency reserves, to a specified extent, would be consolidated and refunded.

Step 5. A multilateral, international gold standard – the result of the conference convertibility agreement – would effectively terminate floating and pegged-undervalued exchange rates. The reformed international monetary system, the true international gold standard, would establish and uphold stable exchange rates and free and fair trade—based upon the mutual convertibility to gold of major national currencies.

Fix Fiscal First

Jerry L. Jordan

"There were no restrictions remaining on the power of governments to finance unlimited debt.... None of this was true under a gold standard."

— Father Robert Sirico[1]

Fiscal fiascos are everywhere. Countries, provinces, states, and municipalities around the world have increasingly paid for current goods and services by issuing claims to *future* tax receipts, rather than current tax collections. In recent decades governments at all levels also have compensated current government workers, in part, by promising ever-more generous retirement pensions and medical benefits, also to be paid by claims on future tax receipts. For even longer the US government has been promising most citizens that they will receive a pension and medical care to be paid out of the paycheck of a younger worker. None of these trends is sustainable.

If there is a silver lining to the 2008 financial crisis it is that the folly of such fiscal regimes has been revealed in bold headlines and vivid video footage much sooner than otherwise. Nevertheless, in spite of much noise and political posturing, policymakers have yet to "stop digging."

Already, the current stock of those claims to future tax receipts—outstanding government debts—together with the current deficits that continue to add to the outstanding debt and the unfunded or under-funded promises of future pension payments and medical care, add up to far more than any tax system can possibly yield. As Allan Meltzer said two years ago, "There isn't going to be enough money in the world in the years to come to finance the U.S. budget deficits."[2]

I can write into my Last Will and Testament, a legal document, that upon my death the executor is to give to each of my three children a 40% share of my estate and to divide the remainder equally

---

1 President of the Acton Institute in Grand Rapids, Mich. "The Vatican's Monetary Wisdom" *Wall Street Journal*, October 27, 2011

2 Interview in Financial Intelligence Report, MoneyNews.com, Vol. 7, no. 12, December, 2009.

among my five granddaughters. The fact that it cannot be done will not be my problem, which appears to be the thinking of many past and present politicians.

Some Propositions

Just as the existence of central banks with discretionary powers to create fiat monies implies that moral hazard is present in the financial system, the absence of binding constraints on the discretion of fiscal authorities creates moral hazard throughout the economy.[3] The fiscal *discipline* that was imposed by convertibility was the virtue of the pre-1914 true gold standard, and to a lesser extent the gold-exchange standard (1946-1973). In a fiat currency world, monetary policy is a fiscal instrument—a way to finance government.

In an *actuarial* sense, government budgets are always balanced; the burden of taxation is measured by *government spending.* All spending is paid by current or future *explicit* taxation, or *implicit* taxation through debasement of the currency. The corollary is that *real tax cuts* can only come through a reduction of spending by government; and only then do you create the conditions for monetary stability. A society that is unwilling or unable to achieve and maintain fiscal discipline will be unwilling to maintain monetary discipline. Without effective institutional limitations, politicians always vote for more current spending, and greater commitments to spend in the future, than any tax structure can support.[4]

---

3 The recent filling of bankruptcy of the city of Harrisburg, PA, demonstrates how pervasive the problem is. "There's no way [state] legislators are going to sit up there and let the capital city of this state go under. They would be the laughingstock of the country," council member Gloria Martin-Roberts said earlier this year. *Wall Street Journal* 10/28/11; Steve Malanga, "How Harrisburg Borrowed Itself Into Bankruptcy."

4 Bordo, Markiewicz and Jonung, "If there are strong fiscal interdependencies between sub-national jurisdictions policy-makers might face incentives to increase their expenditure while externalising the cost to the others. Rodden (2004, 2006) argues that this incentive is higher if the central government cannot *fully commit to a no-bailout rule.* Furthermore, the central government's commitment becomes less credible if sub-central governments are heavily dependent on transfers from the central authority. Intergovernmental transfers, *as opposed to local taxation,* change beliefs about the levels of local expenditure that can be sustained by creating the perception that the central government will ultimately provide financial help. Transfer dependent local governments usually face weaker incentives for responsible fiscal behaviour." [emphasis added]

Sixty-five years of Failed Fiscal Discipline

The post-WW II system known as "Bretton Woods" is usually discussed as a monetary regime or an exchange-rate regime. Aside from the debates about the periods of apparent success and ultimate failure in those contexts, Bretton Woods failed to assure essential *fiscal* discipline. Similarly, the Maastricht treaty that created the euro is usually referred to as a monetary system for Europe, but its fatal flaw was ineffective *fiscal* rules.

After WWI, major countries attempted to return to pre-war gold parities. That flawed and ultimately failed idea contributed to the economic dislocations that precipitated the 1930s economic depression and ensuing political upheavals. The designers of the monetary arrangements after the second world war sought to avoid repeating those errors by making the US dollar the 'reserve currency' to which other currencies would be pegged and the dollar would be the only one directly defined in terms of gold. Under this gold-exchange-standard, the US enjoyed what Charles de Gaulle[5] called the "exorbitant privilege"[6] of borrowing in its own currency. That is, for much of the second half of the past century, only the US was able to sell to foreign official and private investors securities that were denominated in its own currency—US dollars. The commitment of the US government to exchange surplus dollars held by foreigners into gold—it was illegal for Americans to even own gold!—implied that a fiscal discipline needed to be maintained by US politicians.

US Experience—For many years the US Treasury was able to count on placing low-coupon, non-marketable, dollar-denominated bonds with foreign central banks (notably, Germany and Japan) which desired to accumulate 'foreign reserves.' However, by the 1960s the US began to abuse the privilege of borrowing in its own currency by running larger budgetary deficits (Vietnam and the 'Great Society') and supplying more dollar-denominated bonds than the world wanted to acquire. President Johnson would not support proposals for increased taxes to reduce deficits because he did not want Congress to debate the merits of the spending for the

---

5 Some scholars attribute the quote to Valéry Giscard d'Estaing, the French Minister of Finance under de Gaulle.

6 The phrase has sometimes been translated as "extraordinary privilege."

military and social programs. "Guns and butter" were financed by accumulating debt.

By mid-decade, emerging inflationary pressures in the US were eroding the real value of the growing stocks of dollar-denominated bonds held by central banks and governments around the world. One large holder, Germany, faced upward pressure on its currency, yet refrained from seeking gold in exchange for surplus dollars (it was only 20 years since the end of the war), but other countries challenged the Johnson administration to honor the commitment to absorb the surplus dollars in exchange for gold.

Rather than constrain the creation of excess dollar-denominated bonds by reducing spending or raising taxes, the Johnson administration chose capital controls, taxation of foreign travel by its citizens, and subsidies to exporters as temporary measures to address the imbalance between supply and demand for dollars. First suspension, then termination of the 'London gold pool,' and in 1968 ending the gold-backing of Federal Reserve Notes (and with the help of 'moral suasion' on foreign governments) prolonged the period that the US dollar was notionally—but not really—convertible into gold at $35/oz.

A brief lurch toward fiscal discipline in the final year of the failing Johnson presidency in the form of a10% surtax on personal and business incomes helped temporarily to stabilize the exchange regime (aided by revaluation of the German currency). However, the mild 'saucer-shaped' recession of 1970 in the US precipitated "pedal to the metal" monetary policy as 1971 got underway and the world was once again flooded with excess dollars.

By mid-1971, US policymakers faced a dilemma: (1) continue with highly expansionary monetary and fiscal policies and face both continued international pressures to convert surplus foreign-held dollars into a dwindling gold supply, as well as accelerating inflation in the following Presidential election year, or (2) curtail monetary growth and fiscal deficits and risk a return to recession during the election cycle. They chose instead the "magic wand" of floating the currency and imposing wage and price controls which allowed them to open further the monetary and fiscal spigots. The post-election result was first accelerating inflation and a falling dollar and final collapse of the Bretton Woods system, then another lurch toward restraint and a worse recession.

Just a few years later the rest-of-the-world again challenged the US to restore fiscal and monetary discipline during the failed presidency of Jimmy Carter. The US "exorbitant privilege" was revoked in 1978 when foreign governments and central banks demanded that the US issue "Carter bonds"—bonds denominated in the German and Swiss currencies. For the first time in decades the ability of the US to service additional debts would not be based on tax collections or on additional liabilities of its central bank, but on the earnings from exports and proceeds from foreign inflows.

This externally imposed discipline ushered in the 'Great Moderation,' a period characterized by falling budget deficits (and even occasional surpluses), falling inflation, and rapid economic growth. Regrettably, this era did not last into the new millennium.

Foreign Experience—for the first few decades in the second half of the past century, maintaining fiscal discipline was not much of a challenge for most countries outside the US. There was no foreign market for their bonds denominated in their own currencies, bonds denominated in a foreign currency (the dollar) had to be limited by their ability to earn foreign currency, the domestic market for government bonds was limited by the tax systems' potential for generating revenue, and domestic banks were too small to fund large deficits.

Those countries that force-fed debt to their central and commercial banks—especially Latin America, but also a few in Europe—experienced recurring bouts of inflation and devaluations of their currency. Those countries that maintained fiscal discipline and sought to hold domestic inflation below that of the reserve-currency country faced the prospect of periodic revaluations of, or persistent appreciation of, their currency. The associated domestic political pressures (from exporting and import-competing industries) generated by the pursuit of sound money policies meant that the US inflation rate tended to be the floor rate for the world. As this was unacceptable to many people and their elected leaders, the search for alternative monetary arrangements and exchange-rate mechanisms was well underway only three decades after the adoption of Bretton Woods.

A number of interim approaches to new monetary arrangements outside the US preceded the Maastricht Treaty—the bold human design to create a new, multi-country currency for Europe. The architects of the euro knew very well that institutionalized fiscal discipline was essential to the long-term success of this new currency. The treaty required that adopting countries maintain deficits of no more than 3% of GDP and national debt of no more than 60% of GDP.[7] It was the *failure to adhere to these fiscal rules* that undermined the entire common currency project.

As summarized by Bordo, et. al.,

> ... a setup of a single monetary authority and numerous fiscal authorities requires binding fiscal policy constraints to avoid excessive deficits at the sub-central level, that is on the level of the member states in the case of the euro area. Default by a subnational government can impose a negative externality upon other subnational governments or the federal government by increasing the cost of borrowing for all fiscal units. An important question that arises in these circumstances is the impact of effective discipline on borrowing that is imposed by the market. These market forces can work efficiently only if subnational governments have no perceived chance of a bailout by the central government (or the central bank). ... [And] expectations of a bailout are the most important reason for the failure of market discipline. If a bailout occurs, it might disturb or even destroy completely market forces that prevent fiscal units from over-borrowing.[8]

Some advocates of the euro project—especially representatives from countries with chronic fiscal and monetary fiascos, such as Italy—believed that using a currency supplied by Frankfurt would require their own country to become more fiscally responsible. Essentially, they believed that the new euro would operate as a de facto *paper gold standard,* limiting the deficits and debt accumulation of their countries, in addition to assuring low inflation.

However, politicians at all levels of government in a number of

---

7 These provisions were not adequate at the outset. Every country in the euro zone has massive unfunded promises of retirement and medical payments and rapidly aging populations. Jagadeesh Gokhale, Measuring the Unfunded Obligations of European Countries, http://www.ncpa.org/pub/st319

8 Bordo... p. 6

the countries saw that the move away from a domestically furnished currency liberated them from the constraint of incurring debts that must be serviced by their own tax base. Foreign creditors implicitly assumed that counter-party risk was no longer an issue—interest rate differentials throughout the euro zone converged toward the yields on German instruments.

Euro skeptics argued that Rome might feel constrained by the treaty provisions for limits on deficits and debts, but the provinces and municipalities certainly did not. In fact, at the time of the adoption of the euro, Rome did not even have a database that would allow policy makers to know the aggregate amount of euro debt that was being incurred. As it has turned out, this problem was even worse in several other countries, especially Greece and Spain.[9]

Like the Latin America debt crisis of the 1980s, loans made by international banking organizations have been a big part of the build up of the debts and the pressures to socialize the debts in Europe. Had the debtor countries (including provinces and municipalities) been constrained to borrow from foreign creditors only in the form of marketable bonds, there would have been greater transparency about the total amount of such debt and more objective assessments about the ability of the borrower to service such debt. However, the total amount of euro-denominated loans by international banks to all levels of government in Europe was far more difficult to obtain.

While the taxpayers/citizens of a debtor country may be equally willing to default on loans from foreign banks as other foreign bondholders, politicians in the creditor countries are subject to different pressures from the stockholders and depositors of their banks than from other bondholders. Greek citizens don't vote in German elections, but the lending banks' stockholders and depositors do, along side the rest of German taxpayers. This moral hazard stems largely from the glaring ineffectiveness of the fiscal discipline required by the Maastricht Treaty. The borrowers—not the lenders—were supposed to be constrained.

---

9 *Financial Times.* 'Hidden' debt raises Spain bond fears" By Victor Mallet in Madrid, "In fact there are about 5,200 regional and local entities with indebtedness that is not included in the official accounts, amounting to some £26.4bn," http://www.ft.com/cms/s/0/6e89358c-7fee-11e0-b018-00144feabdco.html#axzz1dzQTxHMR

Again like the Latin American debt crisis, when there are no effective limitations placed on the borrowers, and if there are not effective constraints on (nor even information about) the total amount lent, it is not at all surprising that (all too frequently) it is discovered that the outstanding claims to future tax revenues adds up to more than the economy can generate. In economic terms, it is not a question about whether the losses can be avoided; they cannot. The political questions are all about who will incur the losses. Up to a point, the citizens/consumers of debtor countries will incur real wealth reductions. Second, the shareholders/investors of the lending institutions and other bond-holders have incurred real wealth losses that must be realized by writing down net worth. Finally, the consumers/taxpayers of creditor countries who had no part in either the borrowing or the lending will also incur real wealth losses—probably reflected in lower after-tax paychecks or after-inflation real income. The determination of the shares borne by each of these groups is all political.

Menu of Reform Ideas

James Madison's question, "But what is to ensure the inflexible adherence of the Legislative Ensurer to their own principles and purposes?"[10] has not yet been answered. In the past century, all forms of institutionalized restraint on the size and scope of governments—limitations on their current expenditures and on their promises of future payments—have been tested and failed. Constitutions, treaties, statutes, and specie-standards for currencies have all been pushed aside, repealed, revoked, or simply ignored.

Proposals for answering Madison's question range from simply trying again to put teeth into previous approaches, to bolder ideas that are new and even global. Some ambitious ideas call for grand human design requiring major international consultation, cooperation, and even treaties. Less ambitious ideas would rely on the competition of human actions that would result from the end of central bank monopolies of currency.

---

10 Madison, James. Letter to Mr. Teachle, March 15, 1831.

Strengthen Monetary Discipline?

Madison's default position for the new United States was sub-optimal: reliance on specie-backed currency until binding fiscal discipline could be assured. Two centuries later a return to some form of "gold standard" for national currencies still has vocal adherents. The fact that for any one country—even the US—to unilaterally define its currency in terms of specie is not possible, leaves proponents with many unanswered questions about how a return to convertibility of existing central bank notes, bank deposits and debt obligations could be accomplished, and what the enforcement mechanisms would be when a major country finds it to be inconvenient to honor its commitments.

It is probable that accelerating world inflation will give rise to calls for another "Gold Commission," only next time it will be international and will not be limited to reintroduction of specie backing of currencies. Suggestions of currencies "pegged" to baskets of commodities do not address the inherited fiscal imbalances and legacy stocks of debt. Using the "price of gold" or other commodities as 'indicator variables' to tell the policymakers when they need to 'tighten' or 'ease' the stance of policy are useless. Fiscal policies will ultimately dominate; the fiscal foundations of any potential new global monetary arrangements would have to prove more effective than the failed fiscal provisions of the Maastricht Treaty.

The untenable position of central banks is becoming more apparent. Without the ability to estimate even within a wide range how many "dollars" an individual or business will be required to remit to the taxing authorities at various dates in the future, the essential balancing of the demand for and supply of the central banks liabilities is elusive, at best. As a reply to Meltzer's assertion about "not enough dollars," one study[11] retorted that if the share of the rest-of-the-world GDP held in US Treasury securities quadruples from 5% to almost 20%, and/or the Federal Reserve monetizes more but inflation and interest rate increases are modest, then the US base-line

---

11 "Financing U.S. Debt: Is There Enough Money in the World – and At What Cost?" John Kitchen, U.S. Department of the Treasury and Menzie D. Chinn, Professor, La Follette School of Public Affairs and Department of Economics at the University of Wisconsin-Madison; La Follette School Working Paper No. 2010-015

deficits can still be funded by the end of the current decade. Beyond that, individual and business income-based tax rates would necessarily soar to rates that are anybody's guess. Or, debt monetization on a massive scale becomes the politically "least bad" alternative.

The only accurate answer to questions about which of the various estimates of the tens of trillions of dollars of "unfunded entitlement liabilities" is most reliable is: none of them can happen, so it doesn't matter. This is arithmetic, not economics.

Fiscal Reforms

In the US there is renewed interest in various forms of "balanced budget amendments," and/or spending limitations, and ultimate repeal of 16th amendment (substitution of expenditure-based taxation for earned-income-based taxation at the Federal level). Because the 16th amendment allows each Congress to establish the rates at which future taxable income—somehow defined—will be taxed, but one Congress cannot bind the next one, it is impossible for anyone to have more than only a very vague idea of what their future tax liability will be.

Thirty years ago advocates of balance budget amendments soon found that traps could be laid wherein the implementing statutes could require large tax increases if enough of the budget is "off limits" to spending cuts. Or, the budget might ultimately be balanced but as a share of the economy that is much too large and suppresses incentives for economic growth. Also, concerns soon surfaced that the judicial branch of government could mandate tax increases if the legislative branch did not authorize sufficient revenue raising measures. In more recent years, budget analysts have raised questions about how deficits or losses incurred by GSEs[12] would be treated and whether Federal guarantees (think Solyndra) would become even more common and a greater problem.

Opponents of proposals for amendments requiring balanced federal budgets began arguing for separate "capital expenditure budgets" that would be financed with debt, much like state government 'infrastructure projects.' Economists might see the merits of financing the construction of nuclear-powered aircraft carriers with bond

---

12 Government Sponsored Enterprises such as the US Postal Service, Fannie and Freddie

issuance rather than current taxes. However, arguments that "investment in human capital" (that is, for education) should be bond financed, or that expenditures for "protecting the environment" or providing for "homeland security" all provide long-term benefits and therefore should be financed with long-term debt, opens the door to the slippery slope of ineffectiveness. Finally, older versions of amendment proposals had the effect of locking in the inherited national debt because there was no provision for surpluses to pay down the legacy debt.

More recent versions of balanced budget amendments usually contain a component of spending and/or tax limitation, either in terms of growth rates of spending or capping spending as a share of national income, somehow defined. They also exclude repayment of principal on the inherited debt from the balancing requirement; this is important because periods of rapid economic growth are likely to generate tax revenue in excess of projections and thus could be used for debt retirement rather than force tax cuts. In that sense, the intent is to permit budget surpluses, but not deficits, in most circumstances.

The effectiveness of ideas for preventing court-mandated tax increases, or for constraining legislative actions that declare certain expenditures "off budget" and therefore debt financed, is unknowable until tested. Also, at least some proponents of constitutionally mandated fiscal discipline understand that the implementing statutes must also address the actuarial deficits of the legacy "entitlement programs." That is, the pre-existing programs that promise future nominal payments for retirement and for medical services—to be paid out of future tax revenues—cannot continue once spending and taxation are capped as a share of the national income.

The politics of formulating and implementing sweeping fiscal reforms are beyond the expertise of economists. The applause lines, "balance the budget" and "cut, cap and balance" do not make it clear that fundamental reforms of taxpayer-financed pension and medical programs are essential to successful implementation of a constitutional requirement of balanced federal budgets.

A further challenge to the effectiveness of constitutionally-mandated budget balancing at the Federal level of government would be provisions that strictly limit Federal mandates of programs to be implemented and funded by state and local units of government. While these lower levels of government are prohibited from incurring budgetary deficits, many have nonetheless accumulated significant debts as a result of bond issuance for various projects and many have actuarial deficits in their public-employee pension systems. Some state legislatures would no doubt oppose spending limitation at the Federal level once they realize that transfers they currently receive would be curtailed.

On-going Debate

Within the European Union, the disparity of fiscal performance among the member countries has become has become a major political issue. The failure of the fiscal provisions of the Maastrict Treaty are becoming more widely understood. Unfortunately, many politicians and pundits remain hopeful that a central bank—the ECB—can correct the mistakes of the rest of government. Within the US, there has been some progress in improving fiscal performance at the state level, while the fiscal performance at the Federal level has emerged as a seemingly unmanageable problem. Because there is no institutional fiscal discipline, maintaining monetary discipline is doubtful.

The prevailing political model wherein public employee unions (and other large constituent unions such as the AARP in the US) collect dues from members which are donated to the political campaigns of elected leaders who vote to increase/protect payments of taxpayer money to such members must be reformed.

Summation

If debt-financed government expenditures and payments for unfunded 'entitlements' can somehow be eliminated or kept to a minimum over time, then the risk of the "unlegislated tax" of inflation is substantially reduced. Fiscal discipline is a necessary—but not sufficient—condition for achieving and maintaining monetary discipline and financial system stability.

References

© 2011 by Michael D. Bordo, Agnieszka Markiewicz, and Lars Jonung.
"A FISCAL UNION FOR THE EURO: SOME LESSONS FROM HISTORY"
Working Paper 17380, September 2011
NATIONAL BUREAU OF ECONOMIC RESEARCH

Jonathan A. Rodden, "Achieving fiscal discipline in federations: Germany and the EMU", paper prepared for "Fiscal policy in EMU: New Issues and Challenges", workshop organized by European Commission, Brussels, 12 November 2004.

Jonathan A. Rodden, "Hamilton's paradox. The promise and peril of fiscal federalism," Cambridge University Press, New York. (2006)

James Madison, ([1831b) 1953) "[Letter] to Mr. Teachle." In S. K. Padover (ed.) *The Complete Madison: His Basic Writings.* New York: Harper and Bros.

Money's Muffled Message

Sean Fieler

While policy makers are still behaving as if we can go back to the world as it was prior to the summer of 2007—that the right mix of stimulus and enough time will return things to the way they were prior to the crisis—there is a growing recognition in society not only that the Great Moderation is over but that we can't go back—an understanding that we cannot recover the innocent faith that underpinned markets just four short years ago. For the Great Moderation was, more than any other factor, predicated on an abiding faith in the power of government to compress the full range of economic possibilities into a tolerable subset of outcomes. This view is clearly incompatible with a world in which developed-country government debt and, more insidiously, its government-mandated zero-risk weighting, have become the primary sources of economic instability.

With the spell of the Great Moderation finally breaking, society is beginning to publicly and earnestly question the assumptions implicit in our economy. This newfound spirit is catching on not just on Wall Street, the metaphor, but actually *on* Wall Street, the street—the difference being that while those of us in offices are still questioning the risk-free treatment of sovereign debt, those in the streets are questioning the American social contract.

We're all familiar with America's unique version of the social contract—work hard and get ahead. Many of us bear personal witness to the benefits of this system and are grateful to our fellow Americans for not begrudging us our success. That Americans, as a people, have a much greater tolerance for inequality and are less prone to envy than other nations is not an unproven assertion or romantic ideal. It is a well-documented fact. In a recent joint study[1] of the OECD countries, conducted by Brookings and the American Enterprise Institute, Americans remained far and away the most willing to accept economic inequality. Sixty-nine percent of Americans agreed with the statement that "people get rewarded for their intelligence and skill" – a figure that compares with an average of 39% of

---

1 http://www.economicmobility.org/assets/pdfs/EMP%20American%20Dream%20Report.pdf

respondents in the OECD. The corollary to this view, of course, is that only 33% of Americans agreed with the statement that "it is the responsibility of government to reduce inequality" — a figure that compares with an average response in the OECD of 69%.

But, as we all are rediscovering, America's unique social contract of earned success did not arise out of an abstract willingness to elevate the smartest and most determined amongst us. Our system of earned success arose because the large middle class, unique to America since our founding, has benefited from the opportunities our system offers. The average guy, or even the little guy, is sufficiently well off, that with hard work, he too, can get ahead. Or, as Tocqueville so eloquently put it almost one hundred and eighty years ago, "In America I found no citizen so poor that he did not gaze with hope and longing upon the pleasures of the rich, or that his imagination did not savor in advance goods that fate obstinately refused to grant him."[2] While no one doubts that the brightest and the most determined have continued to excel in America, the average family has fallen behind to the point that pleasures of the rich risk engendering more resentment than hope and longing.

Now, I recognize the notion that the middle class has been struggling for forty years will surprise many. After all, the more than five-fold increase in the median income of the American household since 1971, from $9,000 to $50,000 per year[3], certainly provides the clear appearance of progress. But, after factoring in the dollar's 82% loss of purchasing power over the same period, the median household income only rose 16%.[4] And, this much more modest increase is largely the result of the growing prevalence of two-income households. The median real income for working men over the same forty-year period rose just 6%,[5] and that improvement only accrued to the rapidly shrinking percentage of men fortunate enough to still have full-time jobs, just 66% according to the latest data from the Bureau of Labor Statistics, the lowest level on record since the figure was first recorded in 1948.[6]

2   Tocqueville, Alexis de Democracy in America p.618

3   http://www.census.gov/hhes/www/income/data/historical/household/index.html

4   http://www.census.gov/prod/2010pubs/p60-238.pdf

5   Ibid

6   http://www.bls.gov/news.release/pdf/empsit.pdf

Accounting for this involuntary reduction of the percentage of men in the labor force, the real median earnings for all men in their prime working years has declined 27% since 1971 and, predictably, the outcomes for less-educated men have been much worse. The real median earnings for men that stopped their education at high school have halved, down 47%, over the same period.[7]

This shocking deterioration in real earnings obviously started long before the financial crisis of 2008, but not until the crisis of 2008 and subsequent anemic recovery crystallized the trend—clarifying in the mind of many Americans that the solution is not around the corner—did this economic phenomenon turn into a social phenomenon. The social contract is being questioned.

Now, those of us who would like to preserve the American social contract of earned success, and to stop the fundamental transformation of America, need do only one thing: grow the American middle class. This will be no easy task. The two principal forces buffeting the middle class are technology and globalization. Technology, most notably the computer, has put an ever-growing premium on highly skilled labor. Globalization has depressed the wage rates of unskilled Americans, as jobs requiring less skill have moved abroad.[8]

Now, the solution is obviously not to roll back either technology or globalization. The solution, as it has always been, is to adapt. America went from a rural to urban nation, from peace to war, from expansion to depression and back again, and the American people adapted. The real question is, why didn't the American middle class adapt this time as they always have in the past?

Federal Reserve Chairman Ben Bernanke has suggested that our K-12 educational system, which poorly serves a substantial portion of our population,[9] is to blame for the middle class' failure to respond. While this line of reasoning—that people must be better educated, trained and directed—fits perfectly into the world view of a central planner, our poorly performing public schools have little to do with why Americans aren't competing. Ironically, the real reason

---

7 http://www.hamiltonproject.org/files/downloads_and_links/07_milken_greenstone_looney.pdf

8 http://www.kansascityfed.org/publicat/sympos/1994/s94krugm.pdf

9 http://www.federalreserve.gov/newsevents/speech/bernanke20110826a.htm

why the American middle class is becoming less competitive has more to do with our monetary policy than our education policy.

Specifically, by delivering on its oft-stated goal of managing down inflationary expectations, the Federal Reserve baited the American people into using nominal as a proxy for real; and in doing so, encouraged the middle class to mistake the mere appearance of price stability for actual price stability, a mistake in return for which the American middle class received the appearance of progress without its substance.

The question is not "How *did* the Fed do it?" From owner-equivalent rent to hedonic pricing, we know exactly how they did it. The real question is "How *could* they do it?" That so many so highly trained and well-regarded economists, so fastidious about their data and models, could be complicit in such a large deception, defies the credulity of most people.

But most people, judging from the public discussion about the Fed's dual mandate, also seem to be naïve of the principal purpose of the Federal Reserve. Consequently, they lack the skepticism that would come from an understanding of the restriction on truth telling intrinsic to the Federal Reserve's core purpose, preserving financial system stability. Those of us in the financial field, however, will surely appreciate that the stability of a highly leveraged financial system is not compatible with blunt truth telling; we've seen over and over again how quickly leveraged balance sheets translate perception into to reality.

Gold, until 1971, circumscribed the Fed's ability to shade the truth to the short term. It was not until we abandoned redemption that the Fed became vulnerable to a more enduring compromise with the truth. And it was not until Alan Greenspan took the helm that this newfound vulnerability was exploited.

To be clear, Chairman Greenspan did nothing so base as to convince his colleagues at the Federal Reserve to deceive the public; he did something much more ingenious. He put in place models that encouraged his colleagues to believe that it was impossible for them to deceive the public. More specifically, he embedded a false assumption of perfect rationality into the Federal Reserve's thinking, a slight-of-hand that presumed actual inflation would mirror inflationary expectations and consequently transformed the real world task of managing inflation into a largely psychological objective.

With Greenspan's blessing, the imperfect assumption of rational expectations—which already had substantial support within the Fed because of the new modeling it enabled—gained traction. Though he never attempted convincing the Fed, over time, this faulty assumption of rationality, and the models it spawned, trapped the Fed. Captive to its blind faith in both the calculability of reality and the models that perform this calculation, the Fed cannot break free from the system adopted by Chairman Greenspan without proposing an alternative—a constraint that Chairmen Bernanke made clear when he traveled to Princeton a year ago to visit his former colleagues and friends. While reflecting on the constraints of the Fed's models, Chairman Bernanke repeatedly asked his former colleagues to develop new models that relax the faulty assumption of perfect rationality.[10]

While the Fed searches for equations, the reality of rising prices continues to challenge the widely held belief that the price level is broadly stable. The good people of Queens, for example, were well enough grounded in reality to dress down Bill Dudley, the President of the New York Fed, when he ill-advisedly decided to hold forth on the topic of inflation in that borough earlier this year. And, increasingly, the dissidents within the Federal Reserve are more bluntly proclaiming the truth. James Bullard, the President of the St. Louis Fed, leaves little doubt as to where he stands in his recent article entitled, "Measuring Inflation: The Core is Rotten."[11]

With the lie becoming more confusing than convincing, the confused amongst us who accumulated capital during the great debt expansion are now electing to own cash as they wait for the situation to clarify. Yet this is not an option for what remains of the middle class. Having gone backwards for decades, they have little capital left, and they cannot change their careers or skills as some can change their portfolios. And, rightly, they cannot change the sense that they have been deceived and that they were deprived of the one thing they

---

10 http://www.federalreserve.gov/newsevents/speech/bernanke20100924a.htm
11 http://research.stlouisfed.org/publications/review/11/07/bullard.pdf

needed most, the one thing that would have allowed them to adjust, to make the decisions necessary: the truth. Americans need clarity, not the anesthetizing message of the Fed.

Some argue that we can reform the current fiat money system and un-muffle money's message by clarifying the Fed's mission to a single mandate and accurately stating CPI—even managing it to 0%. But not only is this proposal diametrically opposed to the combination of higher inflation and lower interest rates currently favored amongst most policy makers, it is at odds with the Fed's effort to preserve financial system stability. More fundamentally still, it is based on the fantasy that a group of experts will overcome institutional incentives to lie— or become stubborn truth-tellers.

Others, notably Jim Grant and Lew Lehrman, who prefer to deal in reality rather than fantasy, clearly see the problems intrinsic to the current system and argue that we should move directly to the gold standard. They correctly point out that this move would bring discipline back to the system; simultaneously address our fiscal, trade, and savings deficits; and, most importantly, once again make money truthful.

Sound money has also infiltrated the political discourse. Upon examination, however, the sound money rhetoric of the Republican field still contains more of a deep hesitancy about the gold standard than the deep conviction necessary to successfully lead America through a monetary revolution.

A revolution without understanding is risky. Were this contest to unfold today, it would do so before an American people that do not understand the difference between the real gold standard and the flawed imitations used for much of the twentieth century. And this lack of understanding brings with it the risk that gold would be used to prop up rather than revolutionize the current system. Such an outcome would reinforce the notion that successful revolutions, such as the American Revolution, tend to be gradual.

Consequently, just as we ruled ourselves through state government before kicking out the British, we should first seek to reintroduce truthful money state by state. To proceed, the states need only avail themselves of their constitutional right in Article 1, Section

10 of the U.S. Constitution and recognize gold for what it is: money. This recognition that will set in motion a process to completely free gold from taxation and allow it a level playing field to compete against the dollar.

This state-based effort entails no global conference or vote to close the Federal Reserve. Rather, the state-based strategy, which capitalizes on the libertarian impulse running through our society, would achieve its end of honest money through competition rather than force. The best contemporary political analogy for this strategy is found in the post office. The way to close a post office that does little other than waste money and bombard Americans with junk mail is not to run a political campaign against it, but rather, to invent email.

Furthermore, state-lead gold resumption makes sense politically. Asking states to reintroduce gold money is much easier than asking the Federal government to give up its printing press. This may be why it appears to be succeeding. In Utah it is already law[12] (making Utah the safest jurisdiction globally to hold your gold). Beginning with South Carolina next year, other states will follow. With enough states the movement will have the critical momentum needed to pressure the U.S. Treasury to review its patently unconstitutional interpretation that gold is property and not money—the sole remaining national impediment to the broader use of gold as money.

Importantly, this state effort cannot be hi-jacked by the G-20 crowd with their predilection for hopelessly complex systems and elite control. The states do not want to create a new monetary system that they, the states, will control. They want sound money that neither they nor any government can control.

But, lest state-led resumption be viewed simply as a precursor to the broader adoption of the gold standard, let me be clear: state-led resumption will achieve the same goal as the gold standard even if the gold standard is never re-adopted, for it is gold itself as money and not a gold-backed dollar that is the endgame.

The dollar component of the gold dollar is an old technology, and the dollar designation no longer brings something technically useful

---

12 http://le.utah.gov/~2011/bills/hbillint/hb0317so1.htm

to the table. As money goes through technical change—from cows to weighed metal, to coined metal, to milled coins, to paper money, to electronic payment systems—each technological change has brought with it efficiencies with respect to durability, divisibility, portability, and homogeneity—attributes that are all critical to the success of any medium of exchange. And the last technical change, the electronic payment system, has evolved so rapidly that we have yet to fully incorporate it into our thinking about money.

That you no longer need a dollar present to consummate a transaction in dollars, nor physical gold present to consummate a transaction in gold, calls into question the usefulness of the dollar as a designation of a certain weight in gold.

So it is that state-by-state resumption of gold money is actually the direct route to the same end result of gold itself as money—a result that admittedly will not quickly solve the problems of America's middle class, but will, at least, give them a fighting chance to compete in a world that promises to be ever changing.

Sound Money through Free Banking on a Gold Standard

Lawrence H. White

To aim for sound money is to aim for money that is robust rather than fragile, or more technically, money that exhibits only *small and self-correcting* rather than large and cumulative changes in purchasing power. Large changes in purchasing power come from large one-sided shifts in money supply or demand. A sound monetary system is a self-correcting system that minimizes large and uncompensated shifts in money supply or demand. I will argue that free banking on a gold standard is such a self-correcting system. The money we have today is non-commodity-based or fiat money, issued in amounts that depend on the discretion of a committee of central bankers. A central bank issuing fiat money can directly expand the money supply in any amount, unconstrained by any self-correcting mechanism. In nation after nation central banks have expanded to such an extent as to continually erode the purchasing power of the monetary unit. (Central banks also have the power to shrink the fiat money supply, and can indirectly cause major shifts in the public's demand to hold money, but these events have been less common.) The current regime puts our money on an unsound footing.

In the United States today there are two main threats to the soundness of the dollar: the monetary policies of the Federal Reserve System, and the fiscal policies of the Congress and the Presidency.

The Federal Reserve is threatening the reliability of the dollar's purchasing power through its power to expand the money supply, the quantity of readily spendable currency and deposit dollars held by the public (commonly measured by the M1 or MZM stock of money). The Fed directly controls the quantity of the most basic dollars, also known as the monetary base, consisting of bank reserves and Federal Reserve Notes held by the public. The base expands when the Fed creates new base money to buy securities or make loans to banks. The Fed's huge purchases of mortgage-backed securities ("QE1") and Treasury securities ("QE2") have tripled the monetary base since 2008, an unprecedented expansion that (other things equal) portends a steep decline in the purchasing power of the dollar. To date the Fed has diminished the effect of these base expansions on the broader measures of money, and thereby on the consumer price index, by paying banks interest to hold the newly created bank reserves idle rather than to create new deposit balances. The interest rate paid on reserves is the Fed's newest tool for indirectly controlling the volume of deposit balances that the banking system creates for each base dollar. Nonetheless the huge overhang of excess bank reserves undermines the soundness of the dollar by increasing uncertainty about its future value.

The Congress and Presidency are threatening the dollar through budgetary policies that have greatly enlarged the federal debt (relative to their ability to service the debt) and promise to continue enlarging it. For any nation, the United States included, rapidly growing sovereign debt (a continually rising debt-to-GDP ratio) will eventually saturate the market. We can define saturation as the point at which the government's ability to finance additional spending by borrowing comes to an end, because additional current borrowing pushes up the yield demanded by the market so much that the resulting increase in debt service expense entirely consumes the additional amount borrowed. A government that can no longer borrow to cover its current budget deficit, if it cannot immediately reduce the deficit, has only two options left: default on its debt, or print money to pay its bills (and, to the extent that it has borrowed in its own currency, to erode the real value of its debt).[1] To pursue the money-printing option relentlessly is to take the path that leads to hyperinflation.

The phrase "sound money" was popularized in the United States by defenders of the gold standard against inflationist proposals

---

1   The market for Spain's sovereign debt in 2012 appeared to offer an example of (near-) saturation, with each report of anticipated additional borrowing raising sovereign bond yields. News reports noted the Spanish government's "limited ability to raise money." For well-known analyses of how bond financing can max out, so that a given stream of budget deficits can only be financed by printing money, see Thomas J. Sargent and Neil Wallace, "Some Unpleasant Monetarist Arithmetic," *Federal Reserve Bank of Minneapolis Quarterly Review* 5 (Fall 1981), pp. 1-17, and Preston J. Miller and Thomas J. Sargent, "A Reply to Darby," *Federal Reserve* Bank of Minneapolis Quarterly Review 8 (Spring 1984), pp. 21–26. These papers do not consider the option of defaulting. In late 2011 holders of Greek sovereign bonds were compelled to accept a 50 percent writedown that was tantamount to a default.

in the late nineteenth century.[2] In an important later essay in the mid-twentieth century, Ludwig von Mises wrote that the concept of sound money "was devised as an instrument ... against despotic inroads on the part of governments. Ideologically it belongs in the same class with political constitutions and bills of rights."[3] By "despotic inroads" Mises presumably referred to arbitrary violations of rights such as a government: (a) deliberately wiping away existing debts through inflation, whether to favor indebted special-interest groups or to favor the indebted government itself; (b) arbitrarily defaulting on the established contractual obligation of its central bank (or of one or more favored private banks) to redeem its note and deposit liabilities at par in gold or silver (or other reserve money); and (c) using the money printing press to finance an unpopular war.

Mises continued: "The sound money principle has two aspects: it is affirmative in approving the market's choice of a commonly used medium of exchange [historically, a metallic standard]; it is negative in obstructing the government's propensity to meddle with the currency system."[4] The market's choice can be relied upon to be sound, because in the market convergence on a commonly accepted medium of exchange, evolution favors the survival of the fittest. When a barterer adopts indirect exchange, she learns that she can get better deals by offering to pay her trading partners with the commodity or commodities that those traders prefer for their own use as media of exchange. Traders' preferences depend not only on a commodity's popularity – so the convergence is not entirely self-feeding – but also on its relative stability of purchasing power and on physical and market characteristics that make it suitable as a currency (durability, portability, divisibility, uniformity, and the like). Put another way, trade internalizes the benefits to each trader from adopting a medium of exchange widely considered suitable by others.[5]

---

2 For a contemporary definition of sound money see A. Barton Hepburn, *History of Coinage and Currency in the United States and the Perennial Contest for Sound Money* (New York: Macmillan, 1903), pp. 7-8.

3 Ludwig von Mises, "Monetary Reconstruction," an essay that first appeared as Part IV of the 1953 American edition of Mises, *The Theory of Money and Credit* (Indianapolis: Liberty Fund, 1981).

4 Ibid.

5 Lawrence H. White, "Does a Superior Monetary Standard Spontaneously Emerge?," *Journal des Economistes et des Etudes Humaines* 12 (June/September 2002), pp. 269-281.

Because there is no divergence of private from collective interest, there was historically no market failure to produce sound money. Free-market processes produced sound and convenient money when they were allowed to do so. Private mints have produced reputable coins, and private banks have issued reputable banknotes and transaction accounts, when situated in competitive systems under the rule of law. Professor Hans Sennholz summarized the current situation well when he wrote, "Sound money and free banking are not impossible; they are merely illegal."[6]

Money is not on a sound footing when its value depends on having a captive clientele. The principle of sound money therefore also stands against measures to prop up the value of the government's money by restricting the public's freedom to use alternative means of payment – measures such as bans on private gold or silver coinage, burdens on unofficial transfer services, and controls on foreign exchange. In today's fiat money environment the principle of sound money stands in direct opposition to inflationary money-printing policies that tax away the real value of money holdings, and that erode the government's debts to private citizens in real terms, which is the tacit equivalent of government defaulting on its bonds.

Although central bankers vary in their "hawkishness" on inflation, even appointing the best people to run the central bank does not solve the fundamental problems with central banking. Fundamental are (a) the *incentive* problems inherent in the central bank being a branch of the government, and (b) the *knowledge* problem inherent in centrally planning a monetary policy for an entire complex economy.[7]

Politicians appoint central bankers and give them their marching orders. This of course can create incentive problems, for example when – as in Europe and the United States today – the fis-

---

6 Hans F. Sennholz, *Money and Freedom* (Spring Mills, Pa.: Libertarian Press, 1985), p 83.

7 This is not to downgrade the time-inconsistency problem. As Finn E. Kydland and Edward C. Prescott, "Rules Rather than Discretion: The Inconsistency of Optimal Plans," *Journal of Political Economy* 85 (June 1977), pp. 473-92, famously showed, excessive inflation can arise from time-inconsistency (discretion) even in the absence of incentive problems (in their model the central bank perfectly shares the public's preferences) or knowledge problems (in the non-stochastic version of the model, the central bank has perfect control over the inflation rate and knows perfectly well the implications of its chosen rate for unemployment).

cal authorities have huge debts they would like to have monetized. Even supposing a world where well-meaning central bankers enjoy complete independence from political pressure, their pursuit of multiple aims (lower unemployment, higher real growth, more ample liquidity for banks, a stronger or weaker dollar) can lead them to assign second or third priority to the aim of sound money. Their very discretion to shift among policy aims undermines the monetary system's soundness. To make money sound, we must eliminate as thoroughly as we can the power to manipulate it.

The incentive problem is not solved simply by giving the central bank a better mandate. While the Federal Reserve System has only a vague "dual mandate" to balance low inflation against other goals, the European Central Bank has a *constitutional* commitment to aim for price stability (defined as keeping inflation below 2 percent). But the ECB constitution is unfortunately not self-enforcing. In the face of pressure to buy the bonds of heavily indebted Eurozone governments, in order to delay the day of reckoning for Greece (which had to default on its bonds anyway), then Ireland, Portugal, Spain, and Italy, the credibility of the ECB's commitment to low inflation has crumbled. The ECB website continues to declare that "The ECB aims to maintain annual inflation rates as measured by the HICP [Harmonized Index of Consumer Prices] below, but close to, 2% over the medium term," but in practice inflation has risen and remained persistently above 2 percent over the medium term.[8] For "inflation below 2 percent" to be a truly binding commitment, there must be some definite penalty for going astray. The ECB constitution unfortunately does not specify any penalty for ECB decision-makers who deviate from the goal. They do not lose their jobs. This is a fundamental design flaw, with predictable results.[9]

Even supposing that the central bankers were to aim single-mindedly at providing sound money, they inescapably lack the timely and decentralized knowledge they would need to respond

---

8 As of August 2012 the Eurozone inflation rate, as measured by the year-over-year percentage change in the Harmonized Index of Consumer Prices, had been above 2 percent for 20 consecutive months.

9 See Lawrence H. White, "The Euro's Problems are Fundamental," American Institute for Economic Research *Economic Bulletin* (August 2011), www.aier.org/article/2514-euro%E2%80%99s-problems-are-fundamental.

appropriately to changes in the demand to hold money. This is a subspecies of the well-known knowledge problem that rules out dynamically efficient central planning.[10]

The poor track record of the Federal Reserve System

Over its history the Fed has notoriously failed to preserve the purchasing power of the dollar. Before the Fed, silver and gold standards kept the dollar's value roughly constant over the decades. On the Fed's watch, since 1914, the dollar has lost 95.7% of its purchasing power as measured by the Consumer Price Index, most of the loss coming since the closing of the gold window in 1971. A dollar in 2011 bought only as much as 18 cents bought in 1971.[11] Nor has the price level, with chronic inflation, been more predictable under the Fed than before. Someone considering the purchase of a 30- or 50-year bond faces more uncertainly today about the purchasing power of the dollars they will be paid back than an investor faced under the classical gold standard before 1914. That is why the market for 30-year-plus bonds has largely dried up by comparison to the earlier period.[12]

Can we at least give the Fed credit for preventing deflation? We first need to recognize an important distinction that Ben Bernanke neglects: deflation can be good or bad. When productivity increases and, for example, laptop computers become cheaper to produce, it is a *good* thing that their prices are allowed to fall. There is no warrant for expanding the money stock to drive other prices up, so it is a good thing to let the fall in the price of cheaper-to-produce goods bring down the average level of consumer prices. By contrast, when prices fall because people are hoarding money, we have bad deflation. Pre-Fed deflation was mostly good.[13] The Fed's expansionary policy

---

10 For an account of the "socialist calculation debate" see Lawrence H. White, *The Clash of Economic Ideas* (Cambridge: Cambridge University Press, 2012), ch. 2.

11 Author's calculations; CPI data from Lawrence H. Officer and Samuel H. Williamson, "The Annual Consumer Price Index for the United States, 1774-2011," MeasuringWorth 2012, www.measuringworth.com/uscpi/.

12 Benjamin Klein, "Our New Monetary Standard: The Measurement and Effects of Price Uncertainty, 1880-1973," *Economic Inquiry* 13 (December 1975), pp. 461-84.

13 See George Selgin, Less Than Zero: The Case for a Falling Price Level in a Growing Economy (London: IEA, 1997); also Andrew Atkeson and Patrick J. Kehoe, "Deflation and Depression: Is There an Empirical Link?" *American Economic Review* 94 (May 2004): 99–103.

since the 1930s has eliminated episodes of good deflation. But under the Fed's watch there *have* been episodes of bad deflation, most severely in 1930-33 and most recently in 2008-09.

Defenders of the Fed's policy-making might ask: "Although we have given up stability in the purchasing power of money, haven't we gotten something for it, greater stability of real output?" In fact, the statistical record indicates that real output has *not* been more stable, or less variable, under the Fed. The Great Depression, of course, happened on the Fed's watch. The Fed's defenders might say that we shouldn't blame the Fed for that because the Fed's early years were "just practice."[14] But what about the record since World War II? The best statistics that economists used to have said that the postwar period was more stable. But Christina Romer and other economic historians have made improvements to real-output measures for the earlier years. The older statistics were biased toward instability by including only a few commodity series for earlier years, but measuring output more broadly in the postwar period. By itself this contributed to a false impression of improved overall smoothness. With the new measures of real output, the pre-Fed period looks *just as stable* as the post-WWII period. The Fed can't claim that it has improved economic stability on its watch, even if we discard the especially turbulent interwar and Great Depression years.[15]

We see no improvement in real income stability even though the postwar economy is less agricultural and more broadly based, so that we should expect to see improved stability even if the Fed did nothing. By that standard, the Fed has done worse than nothing. The Fed has had a naturally more stable economy to deal with, but under its watch the economy hasn't been any more stable.

A better path to sound money: free banking on a gold standard

The challenge today is to reintroduce constraints on money creation (which will in turn help to put limits on sovereign debt creation) without constraining the ability to meet large shifts in money demand. This is the great, unsolved problem of the post-Bretton

---

14 I owe this tongue-in-cheek characterization to George Selgin.

15 George Selgin, William D. Lastrapes, and Lawrence H. White, "Has the Fed Been a Failure?", *Journal of Macroeconomics* 34 (September 2012).

Woods era. Free banking on a gold (or silver) standard offers a time-tested way. It tailors money supply to money demand without artificially designed rules. Contract and competition compel the mining firms that dig up the precious metals, the private mints that produce coins, and the private banks issue that redeemable notes and transferable account balances, to meet changes in real demand for their products but constrain them not to create an excess supply. There is no problem of designing responsive-but-precommitted policy rules for a monetary central planning committee. The impersonal market process of supply and demand, not any committee or single firm, controls the overall quantity of money. For any region or country, gold reserves can be acquired from the rest of the world when more money is wanted, and sold to the rest of the world when less is wanted. Growth in the global stock of money is governed by market forces in gold mining, rather than by government fiat.

Gold (or silver) as the basic money has the virtue of being issued by no sovereign. When production is as widely dispersed around the globe as it is today, its supply is independent of any sovereign issuer's imprudence, time-inconsistency, or vulnerability to capture by a rent-seeking coalition. The steadiness in the purchasing power of gold over the decades of the classical gold standard is evident from any historical plot of the price level. A basket of consumer goods priced at $100.00 gold dollars in 1879, the year that the US re-fixed the dollar to gold, sold for $100.70 in 1913, the year the Federal Reserve Act was passed. Under the international gold standard the US price level of course reflected the international gold price level. Between the endpoints the price of the basket remained most years in the range between $90 and $102. When it drifted below due to rapid growth in the output of goods (1894-1905), market forces brought it back up. A low price level (high purchasing power of gold) stimulated mine-owners to dig deeper and prospectors to search more widely, increasing new gold output above its usual volume (around 2 percent of the existing stock), which brought the price level back up (purchasing power back down). This was the self-correcting property of a commodity standard in action.[16] The annualized inflation rate over the entire period was a fraction of 1 percent.

---

16 For an exposition of the supply-demand analytics of a gold standard, see Lawrence H. White, *The Theory of Monetary Institutions* (Oxford: Basil Blackwell, 1999), ch. 2.

Critics worry that the purchasing power of money under a gold standard is subject to disturbances from accidental gold discoveries. This is a possibility, but such shocks were historically small and would be even smaller going forward in a world that has now been much more thoroughly prospected. The largest supply shift of the gold standard era, the California gold rush beginning in 1849 (followed soon after by a gold rush in Australia), was smaller than might be guessed. Over the ten years of greatest California gold output, 1849-59, the Consumer Price Index indicates that the price level in the United States cumulatively increased by only 8.8 percent, for an annualized inflation rate of less than 1 percent.[17]

While a gold standard thus does not guarantee *perfect* steadiness in the purchasing power of money, or perfect steadiness in the growth of the money supply, historical comparison shows that in practice it has provided more moderate and steadier money growth, and more stable purchasing power, than fiat money standards.[18]

A gold standard means that a specified amount of gold serves as the economy's numeraire, or unit of account (which amount might be called "one dollar"), and makes gold the "medium of redemption" (bank liabilities are redeemable for gold coins). It does not mean that people commonly make payments by carrying around bags of gold. With a modern competitive banking system, everyday payment media would come in the same formats we use today, namely bank account balances that can be transferred electronically or by paper check, and currency notes. But instead of being fiat money or claims to fiat money, both media would be private commercial bank liabilities redeemable for gold (as they were in most of the world before the advent of central bank note monopolies and demonetization of gold). Because of the private issuers' enforceable contractual obligations to redeem in gold, reputable bank liabilities are accepted as at par, that is, at values commensurate with the gold to which they

---

17 Lawrence H. Officer, "The Annual Consumer Price Index for the United States, 1774-2008," MeasuringWorth, 2009. URL: http://www.measuringworth.org/uscpi/. For more on this and other criticisms of the gold standard see Lawrence H. White, "Is the Gold Standard Still the Gold Standard Among Monetary System?," Cato Institute Briefing Paper 100 (8 Feb. 2008), http://www.cato.org/publications/briefing-paper/is-gold-standard-still-gold-standard-among-monetary-systems.

18 Arthur J. Rolnick and Warren E. Weber, "Money, Inflation, and Output under Fiat and Commodity Standards," Journal of Political Economy 105 (December 1997), pp. 1308-21.

are claims. Because of the issuer's corresponding prudential need to hold gold reserves, the total dollar volume of currency and transferable account balances in such a system—the M1 or MZM stock of money—is geared to the volume of gold.

Free banking – which privatizes the useful functions of the central bank and eliminates the others – makes a gold standard stronger, more durable, and sounder than a gold standard managed by a national central bank. Claims on competing private money issuers have historically proven more trustworthy than claims on sovereign issuers, because only the former claims are enforceable at law (private issuers do not have sovereign immunity from breach-of-contract lawsuits the way a central bank does) and because – absent government guarantees – a bank facing competition must be careful to maintain its reputation if it wishes to attract and retain vigilant depositors and other bank creditors. Maintaining a reputation means meeting all redemption demands promptly, and managing the bank's asset and liability portfolios such that its ability to meet all demands promptly is not doubted.[19] A central bank need not worry about its captive clientele leaving it should it adopt policies that collide with safeguarding redeemability, so it can take the risks inherent in responding to political pressures, for example to cheapen credit or help finance the government's debt. By decentralizing the issue of currency and the holding of gold reserves, displacing central bank monopoly, free banking avoids putting the entire system's redeemability eggs in one basket and eliminates the one institution that can readily loosen or sever the constraints of the gold standard.

The redeemability of notes and account balances, in a competitive environment, effectively constrains the volume of monetary liabilities that the banking system can issue to the level of the demand to hold bank-issued money. Yet it leaves the system able, indeed incentivized, to promptly meet changes in the demand

---

19 George Selgin and Lawrence H. White, "Credible Currency: A Constitutional Perspective", *Constitutional Political Economy* 16 (March 2005), pp. 71-83.

to hold bank-issued money whenever they arise.[20]

Historical problems of credit instability associated with the international gold standard turn out on closer inspection to have been rooted in the national limitation of banking systems, to the concentration of gold reserves in central banks, and to central bank policies that contravened the gold standard's "rules of the game."[21] Problems of financial panics, including those of the greatest banking panic, that of 1929–33, were due to banking regulations that weakened banks. Gold standard countries like Canada, which avoided central banking and the most important sorts of restrictions that weakened banks, avoided panics.

A gold standard does entail the resource costs of mining the gold that is lodged in bank vaults. But every fiat standard known has imposed the deadweight costs of inflation, and the financial "shallowing" effects of variable inflation. The deadweight costs of inflation are the higher transaction costs incurred by people going out of their way to avoid the tax that an ongoing loss of purchasing power levies on the holding of currency notes, and deposits that pay less than a compensating rate of interest. The financial shallowing effects of inflation are lost gains from trade associated with the disappearance of markets in long-term nominal debt instruments, like 30-year bonds, because of the added risk to saver and borrower from reduced predictability of the purchasing power of money units to be repaid in the future. Ironically, the resource costs of gold mining have actually been *higher* since Richard Nixon completed the demonetization of gold in 1971. High and variable inflation has led the public to accumulate gold as an inflation hedge, making the real price of gold (currently around $1700 an ounce) higher than its real price at the end of the gold's monetary era (then nominally $35 an ounce), stimulating more gold mining.

Under free banking, without an artificially imposed high gold

---

20 For details on the money supply process under free banking see Lawrence H. White, *Free Banking in Britain*, 2nd ed. (London: Institute of Economic Affairs, 1995), ch. 1; George A. Selgin *The Theory of Free Banking: Money Supply under Competitive Note Issue* (Lanham, MD.: Rowman & Littlefield, 1988), online at http://oll.libertyfund.org/title/2307; and George A. Selgin and Lawrence H. White, "How Would the Invisible Hand Handle Money?," *Journal of Economic Literature* 32 (December 1994), pp. 1718-49.

21 F. A. Hayek, *Monetary Nationalism and International Stability* [1937] (New York: Augustus M. Kelley, 1971).

reserve ratio, a gold standard would require less gold in the United States than is already currently stockpiled by the US government. The resource costs of a gold standard with free banking are small— smaller than reasonable estimates of the deadweight costs of average fiat-money rates of inflation.[22]

In addition to an overestimate of the resource costs of a commodity standard, the view that an un-backed paper standard (fiat money) with central banking is better than a commodity standard with free banking is often founded on wishful thinking about the artful counter-cyclical management of a paper standard. Keynesian economists view discretionary monetary policy as a way to try to stabilize macroeconomic conditions (smooth out interest rates, output, employment, or inflation). The emphasis should be on "try." In practice stabilization policy has on net been destabilizing. The evidence is fairly clear that its success rate is below the break-even rate even in the United States.[23]

While an ideal counter-cyclical policy can be designed *on the whiteboard* for a central bank assumed to know everything it would need to know to stabilize the economy, in practice that is more knowledge than it is humanly possible for a central bank to have in real time. Despite the best of intentions, the Fed has made inflation higher, distorted interest rates, fueled unsustainable booms, and consequently has made recessions deeper. A gold or silver standard with free banking is more stable *in practice* than the discretionary fiat standards the world has actually seen.

A gold standard with free banking also brings greater fiscal discipline. The Treasury cannot look to a government central bank to absorb new issues of sovereign debt. For the Treasury to borrow, it must commit to repaying in gold, something it cannot print and which no multinational agency can print for it. To find lenders, the Treasury has to make a credible commitment to future budge surpluses sufficient to repay the debt.

---

22 White 1999 op. cit.; Lawrence H. White, "Making the Transition to a New Gold Standard," *Cato Journal* 32 (Spring/Summer 2012), pp. 411-21.

23 Selgin, Lastrapes, and White, op. cit.

Practical advantages of free banking

As mentioned, free banking leaves the provision of everyday media of exchange, currency notes and transferable account balances, to freely competitive commercial banks (coins can be left to competing mints and token issuers). Banks are responsible for holding reserves adequate to meet the redemption demands they face. Balancing the benefits and costs of holding reserves requires banks to make some practical calculations about the public's payment practices, but bankers are good at precisely that sort of thing.

Some critics of central banking and fiat money think it advisable not only to replace them with a gold standard, but also to abolish gold-redeemable banknotes and transferable account balances that are not backed 100% by gold reserves. Checkable accounts could no longer be offered in the form of demandable debt claims backed by fractional reserves, but only as warehousing contracts. It is hard to square such a restriction with consumer sovereignty and freedom of contract. But would a well-informed, non-defrauded customer ever want fractionally backed account balances? Yes. A money warehouse can't pay interest, and must charge storage fees. Fractional reserves enable banks to fund interest-earning loans, and competition then compels them to waive storage fees and pay interest to the account holders. Where the risk of bank default is low enough, a customer may rationally choose the better return, as bank customers did historically. (Those who distrusted banks always had the option of being unbanked and storing money in a vault.) Fractional reserves are necessary for convenient circulating banknotes to exist at all, because a warehouse has no way to assess needed storage fees on a circulating note when it doesn't know who holds the note at any moment.

As a bonus, a system of fractional reserves for bank-issued money economizes on the real quantity of gold tied up in monetary use. It usefully economizes on the resource costs associated with maintaining a gold or silver standard. Adam Smith emphasized this point in *The Wealth of Nations* (1776), and praised fractional-reserve banknotes for speeding Scotland's economic development: "The judicious operations of banking, by substituting paper in the room of a great part of this [circulating stock of] gold and silver, enables the country to convert a great part of this dead stock into active and productive stock; into stock which produces something to the country." Ludwig von Mises agreed with Smith. He noted: "Fiduciary media tap a lucrative source of revenue for their issuer; they enrich both the person that issues them and the community that employs them."[24]

The leading mainstream argument today against free banking is the argument that unrestricted banking is unsound, always ready to collapse. This is the standard argument for the guarantee system known as deposit insurance.[25] Historical experience shows, however, that without government deposit guarantees, without a government central bank to act as an official lender of last resort, and also without legal restrictions that weaken banks, free banking systems are robust. Bank runs have been rare where banks are not artificially weakened and thus failure-prone, because banks are rarely insolvent. Where bank customers have the *option* to run, and are not made inattentive by deposit insurance, banks must behave prudently to attract business. Banks maintained higher capital ratios and held safer asset portfolios than they have since the advent of government deposit insurance. Their assets were better diversified and more liquid. They shied away from excessive default risk, exchange-rate risk, and interest-rate risk (maturity mismatching), in order to assure potential depositors of the bank's low insolvency risk. If necessary, clearinghouse associations provided credible third-party certification of bank solvency and liquidity.

Governments should not undermine banks' efforts to maintain soundness, and should not block market mechanisms that deter and punish unsound banking practices. The histories of banking in Scotland, Canada, Sweden, Switzerland, and many other places show us competitive and stable systems with minimal legal restrictions.[26] As a rule, bank failures, contagion effects, and crises were *less* frequent historically in systems closer to laissez-faire.

24 Adam Smith, *An Inquiry into the Nature and Causes of the Wealth of Nations* [1776], ed. R. H. Campbell, A. S. Skinner, and W. B. Todd (Indianapolis: Liberty*Classics*, 1981), p. 321; Mises, op. cit., p. 359.

25 For an overview of the "inherent instability" view and its critics see White (1999), op. cit., ch. 6.

26 Kevin Dowd, ed., The Experience of Free Banking (London: Routledge, 1992).

Forward, not backward

The pre-Fed system in the United States (the "National Banking System") was far from the best system available because it was far from a free market in banking. Federal regulations hobbled the banks, setting the stage for panics.[27] After the Panic of 1907, Congress convened a National Monetary Commission. They rightly concluded that the system was broken and a serious regime change was needed to improve it. Unfortunately, instead of trying deregulation, they gave us a central bank. We might learn from our failed experiment with the Federal Reserve System; after the Panic of 2007 we might try sound money through free banking: banking without artificial restrictions, privileges, or bailouts; money regulated by free-market forces instead of a central bank.

Sound money would benefit the average citizen by preventing manipulation of the monetary system in the service of special interests. This is not widely appreciated. The financial crisis of 2007-09 led to loud condemnations of free financial and banking competition—based on the mistaken view that what failed was a laissez-faire system—and to applause for central banking and financial regulation—based on the failure to recognize them as the principal causes of the bubble that burst. Congress responded to the crisis not by removing restrictions and privileges from the financial system, but with the Dodd-Frank Wall Street Reform and Consumer Protection Act, a vague 2300-page legislative template that by one count has since its passage "spawned over 6,500 pages of proposed and final rules and regulations."[28] In the insiders' wrangling over what the Act will finally mean, it is hard to believe that the interests of politically well-connected incumbent financial firms will not be served, as they were served by the bailouts given by the US Treasury's Troubled Asset Relief Program and by the Federal Reserve's bad-asset purchases and concessionary loans. In this environment it is well to consider words of wisdom from William Graham Sumner, in his 1896 critique of the naïveté of populists of his day who thought that

---

27 George A. Selgin and Lawrence H. White, "Monetary Reform and the Redemption of National Bank Notes, 1863-1913," *Business History Review* 68 (Summer 1994), pp. 205-43.

28 John Soffronoff, "The Dodd-Frank Act: Size Matters," *Westlaw Journal Derivatives* 18 (9), 16 March 2012, http://newsandinsight.thomsonreuters.com/Securities/Insight/2012/04_-_April/The_Dodd-Frank_Act__Size_matters/

a larger federal regulatory apparatus would deliver them *from* rather *into* the clutches of financial privilege-seekers:

> The parasites on the industrial system flourish whenever the system is complicated. Confusion, disorder, irregularity, uncertainty are the conditions of their growth. The surest means to kill them is to make the currency absolutely simple and absolutely sound. Is it not childish for simple, honest people to set up a currency system which is full of subtleties and mysteries, and then to suppose that they, and not the men of craft and guile, will get the profits of it?[29]

29 William Graham Sumner, "The Free-Coinage Scheme is Impracticable at Every Point" [1896] in Sumner, *The Forgotten Man and Other Essays,* ed. Albert Galloway Keller (New Haven: Yale University Press, 1918), p. 162, online at oll.libertyfund.org/title/2396/226364.

On The Moral Struggle for Sound Money

Alex Chafuen

After an hour-long lecture on money, Ludwig von Mises was asked: "How can we get the United States back on the Gold Standard"? Mises answered: "This is a very important thing and it needs only one thing, it does not need anything else than a change in the public opinion. Today public opinion takes it simply for granted that if the government does not have enough money it prints it." People take for granted that deficits can be addressed by monetary manipulation. Mises then continued: "Why is it permissible for a government to increase the quantity of money? There are many other things which governments are not permitted to do... Government, too, must be subject to definite rules of what is permitted and what is not.[1]"

To convince the public of the negative effects of a particular policy one may make normative, utilitarian, rational, as well as emotional, arguments. This short paper will focus on some of the challenges faced by those who would make a moral case for a return to the Gold Standard—or, a jump forward to a new monetary system with similar characteristics. I will address the declining focus on moral philosophy and examine the current measurements of sound money and monetary freedom used by free-enterprise policy experts.

The Nature of Money

I still recall my classes of monetary economics at the Argentine Catholic University during the mid 1970's. On the first day we started the course with an equation. We also ended the course with an equation. Each class was similar. There was never a class in which we discussed the essence, the nature, or the origin, of money. The key goal of most models and equations was to come up with the optimum rate of monetary creation. Questions about the morality of monetary creation and manipulation were never addressed.

Well, almost never.

My professor of professional ethics at the Catholic University of

---

1   *On Money A Lecture by Ludwig Von Mises*, 1969, http://www.youtube.com/watch?v=-cle9IWPrBBs&t=1h14m54shttp://www.youtube.com/watch?v=cle9IWPrBBs.

Argentina taught us that printing money was "lying, knowing that you are lying and stealing, knowing that you are stealing."[2] But the ethics of monetary policy and its actors occupied merely ten minutes of one class of his course.

I should not be unfair with my *alma mater*; the same was taking place at most universities around the globe. My professors of advanced monetary economics in Argentina were educated in leading universities, and most worked for the Argentine Central Bank. Those who study monetary economics at colleges and universities here will likely seek employment at the Federal Reserve, or at an institution that relies on a good relationship with the Fed.

In fact there is even less focus today on the ethics of monetary policy. J.R. Clark and Dwight R. Lee write in their recent essay, "Markets and Morality," that "as economics became more 'scientific,' positive analysis of the consequences of economic activity increasingly crowded out normative analysis of the morality of that activity." (Clark & Dwight, 2011, p. 1)

Thus it was a big change for me to study monetary economics at my other university, Grove City College. The course was named "Money and Banking" and the main book for the course was *The Theory of Money and Credit* by Ludwig von Mises. This masterpiece of economics begins with a thorough analysis of the nature of money.

Three decades have passed since then. I find myself again fighting in favor of sound money, this time as co-director of the Atlas Economic Research Foundation's Sound Money Project. Some of the challenges we face today are similar to the ones we faced in the '70's, especially the general misunderstanding of economics—the result of many decades of positivist and neo-classical dominance.

Sound Money in the History of Economic Thought

In *Faith and Liberty* (Chafuen, 2003) I provide arguments that complement the writings of Joseph Schumpeter, Raymond De Roover, Murray N. Rothbard, and others who argued that the great moralists of the late middle ages made outstanding contributions to the understanding of economics; most of the first treatises on mon-

---

2   Cayetano Antonio Licciardo (1923–1999) a former Minister of Economics of Argentina.

ey, for example, were written by moral philosophers., The author of *A Treatise on the Origin, Nature Law and Alterations of Money* (Johnson, 2011), Nicolas Oresme (c. 1320-24-1382), was bishop of Lisiuex, France, and studied at the College of Navarre while at the University of Paris. The famous college counted Jean Gerson (1362-1429) as perhaps the most influential late scholastic to pass through its classrooms (he began attending in 1376, when he was just 14). Nicolas Copernicus' treatise on money, *Monetae cudendae ratio* (*On the Minting of Coin* or *On the Striking of Coin*) was published in 1526. Although achieving fame as a scientist, Copernicus had a degree in canon law from the University of Bologna. Father Juan de Mariana, S.J.'s, treatise on the negative effects of monetary debasement, published in 1609, still maintains its relevance. Published originally in Latin and Spanish, it has been recently been translated into English.[3]

Outstanding economists have addressed the philosophical, moral, and social relevance of monetary topics.. For Mises the evil was "philosophical in character. The state of affairs, universally deplored ... was created by a misunderstanding of the nature of money and an incorrect judgment as to the consequences of monetary depreciation" (Mises, 2011, p. 43). Apart from von Mises, Jacque Rueff, in his monumental *L'Ordre Social*, argued that the foundation of the social order of a free society is monetary stability (Chivvis, 2010, p. 105). Rueff is an author who deserves to be brought "back to life." Even Milton Friedman, a great champion of positive, rather than normative, economics, chose to title of one of his books *Money Mischief*—"Mischief" is a word that fits better in the world of ethics than in the sterile world of pure economics.

Sound Money and Relativism

A relativist holds that there are no absolute truths or moral values, but only subjective truths and moral values relative to a particular group or circumstance. In the relativist mindset, finding the truth about money or defining the good and bad in monetary policy becomes an almost useless mental exercise. This essay on sound money is not the place to debunk relativism. "Truth" deals with the

---

3 Juan de Mariana, *A Treatise on the Alteration of Money*, Grand Rapids, Michigan: Acton Institute, 2011.

essence of things; "good or bad" is a concrete, ethical question. Neither fits in the relativist mind set. For those relativists reading this essay the arguments presented are valuable only as they describe accurately the thinking of several groups of actors.

Money is the most commonly used medium of exchange. A means of exchange is a commodity whose economic function is to facilitate the exchange of goods and services. Today, that medium of exchange is "fiat money." *Fiat* derives from the Latin: "let it be done" or it "shall be done." In economics the term *fiat money* usually refers to paper money which is not redeemable or backed by another tangible asset. The term *sound money* refers to a currency which is more conforming to its nature, the latter being "the most widely used means of exchange."

John Maynard Keynes had no problem with *fiat money*: "The Age of State Money was reached when the State claimed the right to declare what thing should answer as money to the current money-of-account—when it claimed the right not only to enforce the dictionary but also to write the dictionary. To-day all civilized money is, beyond the possibility of dispute, chartalist" (Keynes, 2011, p. 5). Carl Menger was less impressed with government-issued tokens, having written that "[m]oney is not an invention of the state. It is not the product of a legislative act. Even the sanction of political authority is not necessary for its existence" (Menger, 2007, p. 261).

We can say the same about other fundamental institutions of the free society; marriage is not an invention of the state. It is not the product of a legislative act. Even the sanction of political authority is not necessary for its existence. Nevertheless, most in our current cultural debates address the topic as if the state and legislature are the ones responsible to determine what money, or what marriage is. For libertarians, removing the state as the final authority to define money might be the most consistent path. Yet, with Article 1, Section 8, of the US Constitution, the Federal government does assert some responsibility.[4]

Judy Shelton, my Co-Director here at the Sound Money Project,

---

4 "To coin Money, regulate the Value thereof, and of foreign Coin, and fix the Standard of Weights and Measures; To provide for the Punishment of counterfeiting the Securities and current Coin of the United States"

examines the topic of culture, and its influence on a potential radical monetary change, in her latest book, *Fixing the Dollar Now: Why US Money Lost its Integrity and How We Can Restore It*. In making her argument, Dr. Shelton employs words and concepts that economists, *per se*, are not trained to analyze: trust, faith, belief. "In terms of political philosophy, it is akin to placing more faith in the wisdom of the free marketplace as expressed in the aggregate decisions of countless individuals than relying on the omniscient judgment of a handful of government-appointed officials" (Shelton, 2011, p.3)

Yet she is mindful of the reality of the situation. Referring to Hayek's statement that "if we ever again are going to have sound money, it will not come from government... it will be issued by private enterprise," Shelton argues that "[t]o attain that level of legitimacy would require going beyond legal definitions or economic comparisons; private money would have to be **culturally** acceptable" (emphasis added) (2011, p. 35). The struggle for sound money, honest money, will not be won with regressions and case studies. Shelton is explicit: "Again, we speak in moral terms when referring to money. This is because the trustworthiness of America's unit of account is a profoundly moral issue. It impacts the value of wages, taxes, savings and investments for hundreds of millions of individuals who make countless decisions based on daily prices. If we can't trust the money, we can hardly believe in the virtues of free enterprise itself" (2011, p. 4).

The Sound Money Remnant?

Those of us who see respect for economic freedom as essential to the preservation of a free society come from very diverse philosophical, family, and cultural backgrounds. Some of us have experienced that diversity in our own lives, shifting positions or growing in our understanding. Many today do not believe that there is much benefit in focusing on understanding the *nature* of things, or that awe-inspiring concept of "objective truth.[5]"

---

5 Although if asked, while most people would answer that they believe in objective truth, in academic circles, the answer would be the opposite. Despite spending a good time in academic circles and being trustee of a university, I belong to the latter group. Be it Ayn Rand's "Objectivism" or Thomistic "Realism" I have always believed that truth, although difficult to know, exists.

I acknowledge that in philosophical debates, those of us who believe in objective truth are in the minority. This makes our battle for sound money more difficult. In this struggle, especially in the United States where her writings have a large following, Ayn Rand's philosophy still motivates and guides many relevant leaders. During this last decade few have played, or will play, a more important role than John Allison. Alan Greenspan, also a Randian, seems to have placed more emphasis on the self-interest part of Rand's philosophy than on her views of objective truth in the arena of money. Allison, during his last presentation at the Cato Institute Monetary conference, continues to be faithful and consistent with the principles espoused by this novelist-philosopher. He is one of the most outspoken critics of the manipulation of money and credit.

Like the protagonists in Ayn Rand's novels, during his career Allison suffered the costs of government impositions. But Allison's focus is not something new, prompted by the latest financial crisis. Those, like Allison, who adhere to the philosophy of Rand, dislike the prevalent pragmatist and positivist philosophies and are instead guided by strong principles. Most are driven by moral rather than utilitarian arguments.

At least in monetary affairs, Allison belongs to the same camp as the late former banking expert, Wesley H. Hillendahl, who wrote that "only when sufficient people recognize the moral nature of the problem and are willing to act accordingly" will the battle for sound money [he spoke of the Gold Standard] have a chance. Sound money "can be accomplished only ... by the predominance of individuals motivated by moral principles and acting with economic responsibility" (Hillendahl, 1974).

The preservation of the current monetary system, based on *fiat,* is possible because it serves the self-interest of many of powerful actors. To win the battle for sound money we will need to inform and inspire the self-interest of others, as well as their moral outrage. Allison does not hide his displeasure: "The Federal Reserve says that they're holding interest rates below market rates. What that means is that they are redistributing wealth from savers to borrowers. That is a very destructive, immoral decision... As interesting as the economic analysis is, I believe that the fundamental fight is over philosophy—over ideas (Allison, 2012, pp. 273-5).

Allison blames the conceit of the monetary authorities on a combination of altruism and pragmatism. He attacks pragmatism on rational and moral grounds: "The problem with being a pragmatist is you can't be rational because rationality requires a long-term perspective. You can't have integrity either, because integrity is acting consistent with principles," and principles must frequently be abandoned to give way to pragmatic solutions. "The central question in our society today that underlies all of these issues, and it relates to sound money is: Do we really believe in personal responsibility or not?" (2012, p. 276).

Measurements of Sound Money Influence our Normative Judgments

Notions of what is good, of what "ought to be," are heavily influenced by our ideas of what "is." So what "is" the state of money today? Measurements in social science are difficult, and measuring sound money is no exception. According to some of the current measurements there are no major problems with our money. Our monetary thermometers, if you will, indicate no fever.

If we were to catalogue the past analyses of currency debasement and artificial monetary creation, I estimate that over 95% of the negative effects mentioned in most papers and books are related to the effects on price inflation. From Copernicus to Juan de Mariana, to Ludwig Von Mises, Hans F. Sennholz, or even Atlas's Antony Fisher, most of the damage described in their works stem from the deleterious effects of the creation of money on prices throughout the economy. It is that change in prices, especially when unanticipated, that then affects contracts, changes real wages, and subverts the relationship between creditors and borrowers; it is a redistribution of wealth from the poor and middle class to the politically connected who have early access to the newly created money.

During the last few years, while the economy has experienced a huge increase in the money supply, there has at the same time been a huge increase in the demand for cash balances, leaving popular measures of price inflation showing little change. This makes the battle for sound money more difficult. The majority of the population perceives no sense of an inflationary crisis. In relevant policy circles experts still caution about the dangers of *deflation*.

Yet the manipulation of money and credit, even where there is no price inflation, still affects market participants. One can make an adequate case for the immorality of inflation by making reference to a class of lenders who did not anticipate monetary expansion, who would then suffer, and a class of borrowers, who would benefit. As von Mises aptly described, when the "class" of creditors was the wealthy, promotion of inflation had a populist, even redistributive, impulse: "let's help the poor debtors." The opposite has been happening for some time. Many times it is the poor classes, or the elderly, which hold a larger proportion of assets in instruments that are less protected against Friedman's *monetary mischief*. It is the well connected who benefit from the "quantitative easing" and the targeted bailouts.

Making a credible case against credit manipulation is more difficult than making a case against the price effects of increase in the money supply. It requires a more elaborate analysis and getting more into specifics. Which banks and credit institutions were benefited, which one suffered? Focusing on price increases, though easier, does not tell the whole story.

At least in the policy battles, many of those who fight for economic freedom tend to rely on the economic freedom indices produced by The Heritage Foundation, and co-published by *The Wall Street Journal* (Heritage), and by The Fraser Institute, co-published by the Cato Institute (Fraser). These indices include measures of "monetary freedom" and "sound money."

The Heritage index value for *monetary freedom* combines a measure of price stability with an assessment of price controls. Inflation is measured not by increases in monetary supply but by increases in the price level. The authors correctly state that "both inflation and price controls distort market activity. Price stability without microeconomic intervention is the ideal state for the free market.[6]"

Quoting directly from the methodology of their index:

> The score for the monetary freedom component is based on two factors: The weighted average inflation rate for the most recent three years and price controls. The weighted average

---

6 The Heritage Foundation in Partnership with Wall Street Journal, "Monetary Freedom" (The Heritage Foundation, 2012), http://www.heritage.org/index/monetary-freedom.

inflation rate for the most recent three years serves as the primary input into an equation that generates the base score for monetary freedom. The extent of price controls is then assessed as a penalty of up to 20 points subtracted from the base score.[7]

The Heritage measurement of monetary freedom focuses more on pricing policy than monetary policy. Over long periods it should capture many of the effects of an inflationary monetary policy, but over the short term the evolution of the index might fail to alert readers of any problem. Heritage uses the price index because it has "been widely considered as an indicator of the effectiveness of government monetary policy that affects price stability."

The Heritage index also measures *financial freedom,* in which they include many elements that influence monetary policy, including assessments of central bank independence and the manner in which it conducts its supervisory and regulatory functions. A large banking sector owned or controlled by governments will also play a role in monetary manipulation and policy. The Heritage index gives low scores of financial freedom to countries whose central banks are not independent and are subject to government influence.

The Fraser index measures access to *sound money.* It includes growth in the money supply, price inflation, and freedom to own foreign currency accounts. The monetary growth component measures the average annual growth of the M1 money supply over the last five years, minus the average annual growth of real GDP over the last ten years. In addition, for the sake of accuracy, those who prepare the Fraser index wait for all of the data to be published. This usually means that the index reflects measurements that are two years old, a drawback for current policy debates.

The price inflation components of the Fraser index measure the standard deviation of the inflation rate over the last five years, and the most recent year's rise in the Consumer Price Index. Countries that achieve perfect price stability earn a rating of 10. As the inflation rate moves toward a 50% annual rate, the rating for this component moves toward zero. A zero rating is assigned to all countries with an inflation rate of 50% or more.

---

7   Ibid.

The Fraser index also assesses "freedom to own foreign currency bank accounts." Where foreign currency bank accounts are permissible, without restrictions both domestically and abroad, the rating was 10; where these accounts are restricted, the rating is zero. If foreign currency bank accounts are permissible domestically but not abroad (or vice versa), the rating is 5.

Rather than including price controls in its sound money measurements, Fraser researchers include them in their *freedom from regulatory burden* area. Independently of these differences, the Heritage Foundation and the Fraser Institute measurements show very high degrees of monetary freedom and sound money and little deterioration. This is the case especially for the larger economies. In

Table 1

Fraser Institute (Max score 10)						
Countries	Money growth	Sound Money 2009	Sound Money 2008	Sound Money 2007	Sound Money 2006	Sound Money 2005
Argentina	7.8	7.0	6.9	7.1	6.2	5.4
Canada	9.6	9.6	9.5	9.5	9.7	9.7
Chile	8.4	9.0	9.2	9.1	9.1	9.3
Germany	8.5	9.5	9.5	9.5	9.5	9.5
Greece	9.1	9.6	9.6	9.6	9.5	9.6
United Kingdom	8.7	9.6	9.4	9.4	9.4	9.4
United States	8.9	9.6	9.7	9.7	9.7	9.8
Venezuela	6.1	5.4	5.3	5.6	5.6	5.1

Heritage (scored over 100)						
Countries	2010	2009	2008	2007	2006	2005
Argentina	60.7	60.6	65.0	71.4	71.5	65.4
Canada	77.3	80.8	81.0	80.7	85.9	84.7
Chile	73.0	77.3	78.8	79.8	87.1	84.4
Greece	77.6	78.0	78.5	78.4	78.7	78.1
United Kingdom	73.7	80.4	80.7	81.3	86.7	85.0
United States	78.1	84.0	88.7	83.8	85.0	85.7
Venezuela	47.7	53.7	60.6	57.6	53.9	51.9

Table 1, I show the scores for selected economies. During this last decade, on a 1-10 score where 10 is the best, the United States and the Euro zone score between 9.3 and 9.5.

Moreover, when studying the Fraser and Heritage indices from their inceptions, it is hard to find an area where there has been a faster move toward "economic freedom" as in monetary affairs.

The trend towards lower inflation around the world started almost immediately after F.A. Hayek published a list about the "Destruction of Paper Money" which had taken place between 1950 and 1975. It appeared with country data in the appendix of his *Denationalization of Money* (Hayek, 1990, p. 136-7) The destruction of the value of paper money in the 60 countries listed by Hayek ranged from 40% to 99%. Several South American countries appeared as the worst: Chile, Uruguay, Argentina, Brazil . . .and several as the best: Venezuela, Guatemala and Panama (which lost 40-45% of the value, beating US and Switzerland, who saw the value of their currency lose 57% during that period).

The economic freedom indices do not yet show any major reversal in the trend towards more freedom in monetary affairs. The Fraser index, which in theory is more focused on money than the Heritage index, which focuses on prices, shows a much better score. If that is the case, why bother to push for sound money? One reason is that even with these current measurements, especially with the Heritage index, we see a negative effect of unsound money on rule of law.

Table 2

	Monetary Freedom	Financial Freedom	Sound Money
Property Rights	0.46	0.74	0.73
Freedom from Corruption	0.42	0.66	0.66
Rule of Law	0.45	0.61	0.70

If we include the Heritage score on financial freedom in the context of sound money with the monetary freedom factor and average both scores to get a new "sound money" indicator, the correlation between Sound Money and Rule of Law is 0.70.

This is a very significant relation.[8] These results confirm assessment that "there is an intimate relationship between money and freedom; between the keeping of promises and the certainty of contracts; between social function and the rule of law" (Frankel, 1997, p. 12).

The manipulation of money and credit, and the methods used today to increase "liquidity," are still the causes of great injustices, enriching some—who get the rescue or the fresh funds from the government—while letting others fail. But to explain these negative effects in a way that might motivate others to action, or generate the moral outrage necessary for a radical change of our monetary system, analysts would need to speak of specific cases. It is not enough to blame "corporate welfare," "crony capitalism," or the "banksters." Sound money advocates should have access to and describe data from the Federal Reserve to show how government, or quasi-government, agencies distributed their favors.

At the time that I am writing this, it is still uncertain whether the vote of 327 to 98 in the US House of Representatives to allow a full audit of the Federal Reserve, including an audit of the Fed's monetary policy decisions, will lead to a *true* audit. Similar audits should take place in the World Bank, International Monetary Fund, Inter-American Development Bank, and other politicized agencies, which, in many cases, have aided the manipulation of money and credit on a grand scale.

Analysts with libertarian and conservative leanings seem to fear that, if they bring to the surface the name of private sector actors who reap profits thanks to their privileged relationship with the government, they might provide ammunition to those who want even more state intervention into the economy. This is a reasonable utilitarian concern, but it is a handicap for those who seek to actively defend the entire free enterprise system, including banking, on *moral* grounds.

---

8 I thank Anthony B. Kim, Heritage Foundation, for preparing this small but relevant table. The Rule of , score in this correlation is an average of the scores of respect for property rights and of freedom from corruption. All the scores are from the 2012 edition of the Index of Economic Freedom. The correlation coefficient is a concept used in statistics. When there is no relationship between the predicted values and the actual values the value is 0. As the strength of the relationship between the predicted values and actual values increases so does the correlation coefficient. A perfect relationship produces a coefficient of 1.0. A correlation of 0.7 is very significant.

The effort to fight corruption provides us with a good analogy. In Latin America and other regions suffering from corruption and from injustices stemming from government granted privileges, many denounce corruption. These denunciations are echoed in the World Bank, IMF, and other bureaucracies. But few mention names and guilty parties. Blaming corruption and crony capitalists in general has helped little to reverse the trend.

Conclusion

"The *raison d'état*, in which collectivist ethics has found its most explicit formulation, knows no other limit than that set by expediency—the suitability of the particular act for the end in view" (Hayek, 2001, p. 166-7). The entire legal framework relevant to monetary creation and monetary policy conforms more to societies run by the "reason of state" than by those willing to conform to a rule of law. Using Keynes' terminology, for a considerable period of time, the state has been writing the dictionary on monetary affairs.

In few other periods of history has the state commanded such an authority over the material wealth and the opinion of voters in the United States. The fact that there are more think tanks, and many more advocates of free-markets and free-enterprise, than some decades ago might create some optimism for the future, yet during the last US presidential election, after a period of excessive growth of the state in economic matters, the electorate chose a president who advocated and put in practice even more interventionism.

This should not have come as a surprise. In discussion of the monetary situation today, the attitude of the one half is that the state has created this mess, so let the state take us out of it; yet for the other half it is unbridled capitalism that has instigated the need more state intervention. Only a small minority seems to reason: "This crisis was brought by state intervention in monetary affairs. Let's get the state out of this area."

Most economists sympathetic to the idea of the free society seem to agree that the problem is more political and philosophical than economic. For Hazlitt, the key question was "how to get the monetary system out of the hands of politicians," concluding that "as long as we retain our nearly omnipotent redistributive State, no sound currency will be possible" (Hazlitt, 1995, p. 178). He was not optimistic that states could be convinced to "voluntarily to repeal their legal tender laws and to surrender their monopoly of money issue. I confess I cannot see precisely how this political problem is going to be solved" (1995, p. 190).

During these times of monetary doubts and credit crises, dissatisfaction with the current system has grown. Yet despite the efforts of philanthropists, policy leaders, and many talented and generous educators, it is sad, or eye-opening, that Ludwig von Mises' conclusion of more than 50 years ago still describes today's reality: "without exception all drafts for an improvement of currency systems assign to the governments unrestricted supremacy in matters of currency and design fantastic images of super privileged super banks. Even the manifest futility of the International Monetary Fund does not deter authors from indulging in dreams about a world bank fertilizing mankind with floods of cheap credit. The inanity of all these plans is not accidental. It is the logical outcome of the social philosophy of their authors." (Mises, 2009).

The road to sound money will require major changes in thinking. Richard Timberlake stated that "the proper monetary policy for the economy is no government connection to money at all" (Timberlake, 1991). To make his dream a reality, a paradigm shift will have to take place in the world of economic thought and in people's attitude towards the role of government.

Juan de Mariana, the courageous Jesuit who described the negative effects of currency debasement more than four centuries ago, argued that the only reason that the government does not steal surreptitiously in other areas as it does in money, is because we do not let the government in. If the government were in charge of the granaries it would also steal our grain. Mariana condemned the abuse of money as a "base crime that is full of great disadvantages" (Mariana, 2011, p. 55), not least because it allows politicians to interfere in all of our acts of economic cooperation (2011).

As von Mises said, to return to sound money we need only one thing: to win the war over public opinion. We will need to do a much better job in documenting the injustices and evil effects of monetary manipulation. We will need to improve measurements of sound money and monetary freedom. We will need to reclaim academia from the patronage and influence of the very institutions that would subvert and distort truth. And we must convince the people of the moral imperative of sound money.

References

Allison, John. "The Fed's Fatal Conceit." *Cato Journal* 32, no. 2 (Spring/Summer 2012).

Branden, Nathaniel. "Common Fallacies About Capitalism." In *Capitalism: The Unknown Ideal*. New York: Signet Book New American Library, 1967.

Chafuen, Alejandro Antonio. *Faith and liberty : the economic thought of the late scholastics*. Lanham, Md.: Lexington Books, 2003.

Chivvis, Christopher. *The monetary conservative : Jacques Rueff and twentieth-century free market thought*. DeKalb: Northern Illinois University Press, 2010.

Clark, J.R., and Dwight Lee. "Markets and Morality." *Cato Journal* 31, no. 1 (Winter 2011): 1–25.

"Constitution of the United States of America-1787", n.d. http://uscode.house.gov/pdf/Organic%20Laws/const.pdf.

Foundation for Economic Education, inc. *Inflation is theft*. Irvington-on-Hudson, N.Y.: Foundation for Economic Education, 1994.

Frankel, S. Herbert. *Two philosophies of money : the conflicts of trust and authority*. New York, NY: St.Martin's Press, 1977.

Friedman, Milton. *Money mischief : episodes in monetary history*. San Diego: Harcourt Brace & Co., 1994.

Hayek, Friedrich A. von. *Denationalisation of money : the argument refined : an analysis of the theory and practice of concurrent currencies*. London: Institute of Economic Affairs, 1990.

Hayek, Friedrich A. von, Peter G Klein, W. W. Bartley, Stephen Kresge, Leif Wenar, Bruce Caldwell, and Lawrence H White. *The collected works of F.A. Hayek*. Chicago: University of Chicago Press, 1989.

Hayek, Friedrich A. von. *The road to serfdom*. London: Routledge, 2001.

Hazlitt, Henry. *The inflation crisis, and how to resolve it*. Irvington-on-Hudson, N.Y.: Foundation for Economic Education, 1995.

Hillendahl, Wesley. "Inflation: Byproduct of Ideologies in Collision." *The Freeman*, July 1974. http://www.thefreemanonline.org/features/inflation-byproduct-of-ideologies-in-collision/.

Hülsmann, Jörg Guido. *The ethics of money production*. Auburn, Ala.: Ludwig von Mises Institute, 2008.

Johnson, Charles, trans. *The De Moneta of Nicholas Oresme and English Mint Documents*. Auburn, Ala.: Ludwig von Mises Institute, 2011. http://mises.org/books/oresme.pdf.

Keynes, John Maynard. *A Treatise on Money*. London: Macmillan, n.d.

Lehrman, Lewis E. *The true gold standard : a monetary reform plan without official reserve currencies : how we get from here to there*. [S.l.]: Lehrman Institute, 2011.

Mariana, Juan de, P. T Brannan, Stephen John Grabill, and Alejandro A Chaufen. *A treatise on the alteration of money*. Grand Rapids, Mich.: Acton Institute, 2011.

Menger, Carl, Peter G Klein, Friedrich A. von Hayek, James Dingwall, and Berthold Frank Hoselitz. *Principles of economics*. Auburn, Ala.: Ludwig von Mises Institute, 2007. http://vforvoluntary.com/principles-of-economics/index.html?chapter8.html.

Von Mises, Ludwig, Percy L Greaves, and Bettina Bien Greaves. *On the manipulation of money and credit : three treatises on trade-cycle theory*. Indianapolis: Liberty Fund, 2011.

Mises, Ludwig Von. *Theory of money and credit*. [S.l.]: Ludwig Von Mises Institut, 2009.

Rothbard, Murray. *What Has Government Done to Our Money?* Larkspur, Colorado: Pine Tree Press, 1964.

Siegan, Bernard H, Centro de Investigación y Estudios Legales (Peru), and Atlas Economic Research Foundation. *Reforma constitucional : esbozando una constitución para una república que emerge a la libertad*. [Lima, Peru: CITEL, 1993.

_____ . *Reforma constitucional : esbozando una constitución para una república que emerge a la libertad*. [Lima, Peru: CITEL, 1993.

The Heritage Foundation in Partnership with Wall Street Journal. "Monetary Freedom". The Heritage Foundation, 2012. http://www.heritage.org/index/monetary-freedom.

Timberlake, Richard Henry, and George Edward Durell Foundation. *Gold, greenbacks, and the Constitution*. Berryville, Va.: George Edward Durell Foundation, 1991

Author Biographies

Gerald P. O'Driscoll Jr. is a senior fellow at the Cato Institute. He is a widely quoted expert on international monetary and financial issues. Previously the director of the Center for International Trade and Economics at the Heritage Foundation, O'Driscoll was senior editor of the annual *Index of Economic Freedom*, co-published by Heritage and *The Wall Street Journal*. He has also served as vice president and director of policy analysis at Citigroup. Before that, he was vice president and economic advisor at the Federal Reserve Bank of Dallas. O'Driscoll has taught at UCSB, Iowa State University and New York University. He is widely published in leading publications, including *The Wall Street Journal*. O'Driscoll holds a B.A. in economics from Fordham University, and an M.A. and Ph.D in economics from UCLA.

Steve H. Hanke is a Professor of Applied Economics and Co-Director of the Institute for Applied Economics, Global Health, and the Study of Business Enterprise at The Johns Hopkins University in Baltimore. Prof. Hanke is also a Senior Fellow at the Cato Institute in Washington, D.C.; a Distinguished Professor at the Universitas Pelita Harapan in Jakarta, Indonesia; a Senior Advisor at the Renmin University of China's International Monetary Research Institute in Beijing; a Special Counselor to the Center for Financial Stability in New York; a member of the National Bank of Kuwait's International Advisory Board (chaired by Sir John Major); a member of the Financial Advisory Council of the United Arab Emirates; and a contributing editor at *Globe Asia* Magazine. Prof. Hanke's most recent books are *Zimbabwe: Hyperinflation to Growth* (2008) and *A Blueprint for a Safe, Sound Georgian Lari* (2010).

Allan H. Meltzer is the Allan H. Meltzer University Professor of Political Economy at Carnegie Mellon University. He is the author of *History of the Federal Reserve, Volumes I and II* (University of Chicago Press, 2002, 2010), a definitive research work on the Federal Reserve System. he is He has been a member of the President's Economic Policy Advisory Board, an acting member of the President's Council of Economic Advisers, and a consultant to the U.S. Treasury Department and the Board of Governors of the Federal

Reserve System. In 1999 and 2000, he served as the chairman of the International Financial Institution Advisory Commission, which was appointed by Congress to review the role of the International Monetary Fund, the World Bank, and other institutions. The author of several books and numerous papers on economic theory and policy, Mr. Meltzer is also a founder of the Shadow Open Market Committee.

George Selgin is professor of economics at the University of Georgia. He is an expert on banking, monetary policy, and macroeconomics. He is author of *Bank Deregulation and Monetary Order, Good Money: Birmingham Button makers, the Royal Mint, and the Beginnings of Modern Coinage, Less Than Zero: The Case for a Falling Price Level in a Growing Economy, and The Theory of Free Banking: Money Supply under Competitive Note Issue*. Dr. Selgin is also a Senior Fellow at the Cato Institute.

Lew Lehrman is Senior Partner at L. E. Lehrman & Co. investment firm. Lehrman has written books and articles on American history, national security, and economic and monetary policy. He has co-authored the book *Money and the Coming World Order*. He has also written on economic, foreign policy and national security issues in publications such as *Harper's, The Washington Post, The New York Times, The Wall Street Journal, National Review, and Policy Review*. He is chairman of The Lehrman Institute, a public policy research and grant making foundation founded in 1972. He has also been a trustee of the American Enterprise Institute, the Morgan Library, the Manhattan Institute and the Heritage Foundation. He is a former Chairman of the Committee on Humanities of the Yale University Council.

Jerry L. Jordan is Senior Fellow of the Fraser Institute, past president of the Federal Reserve bank of Cleveland, and Financial Sustainability, Entrepreneurship and the Common Bank of Cleveland and was a Member of President Reagan's Council of Economic Advisers. This paper was originally prepared for a conference hosted by the Witherspoon Institute, "The Economic Challenge: Fiscal, Monetary Good," Princeton University, December 5 and 6, 2011

Sean Fieler is General Partner of Equinox Partners, LP. He is also chairman of the American Principles Project. He is a board member of the Witherspoon Institute, Institute for American Values, and the Dominican Foundation and President and Chairman of the Chiaroscuro Foundation. He is a board member of the Committee for Monetary Research and Education and regularly advises on financial markets and monetary policy.

Lawrence White is a professor of economics at George Mason University and a Senior Scholar at the Mercatus Center. Prior to his position at George Mason, he was the F. A. Hayek Professor of Economic History in the Department of Economics, University of Missouri-St. Louis. He has been a visiting professor at the Queen's School of Management and Economics, Queen's University of Belfast, and a visiting scholar at the Federal Reserve Bank of Atlanta. He is the author of *The Theory of Monetary Institutions* (Blackwell, 1999), *Free Banking in Britain* (2nd ed., IEA, 1995), and *Competition and Currency* (NYU Press, 1989).

Alex Chafuen is President of the Atlas Economic Research Foundation. He served as President and CEO of Atlas from 1991-2009, and was elected to its Board in 2009. He is also the president and founder of the Hispanic American Center of Economic Research and is the author of *Faith and Liberty*. He serves on the boards of the Chase Foundation, the Acton Institute, and the Fraser Institute. A graduate of the Argentina Catholic University, he was Associate Professor at the Argentine Catholic University, University of Buenos Aires, and The Hispanic American University, CA. He recently became a Trustee for Grove City College, PA.